It's Time
To End
Church
Splits

~Breaking the Curse
~Healing the Wounds
~Possessing Christ's Unoffendable Heart

Francis Frangipane

IT'S TIME TO END CHURCH SPLITS

Arrow Publications
P.O. Box 10102
Cedar Rapids, IA 52410
Phone: (319) 395-7833
Toll Free: (877) 363-6889
Fax: (319) 395-7353
Web Site: http://www.inchristsimage.org

CONTENTS

INTRODUCTION

I have written this book on the premise that Jesus Christ is the same person today as He was in the first century (see Heb 13:8). Just as He prayed that His early disciples would become one, so He also looked forward in time and prayed for our unity today. Remember His prayer? He said,

> I do not ask in behalf of these alone, but for those also who believe in Me through their word; that they may all be one. —John 17:20–21

As a result of Christ's prayer, for me at least, it is not enough to love the Lord; to fulfill my love, I am learning to love what He loves. Dear friend, Jesus passionately loves the church, even in its imperfections. And, He loves pastors, even while they too are not perfect. Indeed, if we could ascend into heaven and were granted grace to look upon the face of Christ and actually ask Him about splits and divisions, I believe the tears in His eyes alone would tell us disunity is the work of hell.

My goal, therefore, is to help shepherds and their flocks secure Christlikeness in their church relationships. Indeed, I believe that Christ expects those who are born again to be united in heart with one another. This means that we must refuse the work of the enemy to divide and destroy our churches. The curse of division has gone on long enough.

How I Compiled These Chapters

To write this book on church splits has been a daunting task. There may be other works available on this subject, but I have not found any. Thus, to help me prioritize what I would put in this book, we asked those who receive our weekly e-mail teaching to comment on the first chapter, which we sent as the weekly message. Most of the responses I received were passionate and heartrending.

Approximately 60 percent of those who responded expressed a deep and ongoing grief because of what they suffered in a church split. Of these, about 25 percent wrote long and painful responses, the majority describing how a discontented group within their congregation divided and split what once was a loving church. A few of these e-mails were so painful they brought tears to my eyes. Within this group, the most common adjective used to describe the experience was the word "devastating."

Quite a few who wrote said they had been through more than one split. Others were children when they experienced the division and now, as adults, they described their extreme difficulty in returning to Christianity. About ten percent were cynical and critical. Their concern was that this might be another book that justified what they called the "abuse of authority." They expressed that their church divided because of the pastor's sin. They also complained that the lack of accountability in a few nondenominational churches let pastors become so authoritarian that the only "spiritual" thing left to do was to rebel and start a new assembly. Citing the Protestant reformers, a handful within this group felt the greatest Christians the church has ever produced were those who confronted ungodly leaders.

Additionally, a number of people presented very complex situations that led to their church splitting. Others simply wanted to know what can be done to find healing, as the wounds of a split remained open within their hearts.

Obviously, no one book could answer all these questions. Even if I tried, I do not think I would have the right answers to each of these situations. So, I have sought to address the most common issues: the splits that are born of ambition in a subordinate pastor or worship leader as well as the splits where the pastor himself divides the church or falls in serious sin. My goal is to help heal the hearts of pastors and congregations alike. I also desire to set some standards, or "kingdom ethics," to help avoid this heartache in the future.

For those who are fearful that I am seeking to unite everyone who calls themselves Christian, I want to remind you that my appeal is to the born-again church. My readers are primarily people who desire to become more Christlike. If you are reading this, but do not desire to become like Jesus, you will probably not get far within these pages.

One last thing: If you are in the midst of a serious church division, I suggest that you review the table of contents and start this book with the chapters that are most relevant to your current situation. Of course, you should return to the unread chapters, but it may be important that you assimilate first the information that addresses your immediate conflict.

With the Lord's help, I will seek to post on our web site at http://www.inchristsimage.org some of your questions together with my corresponding advice. Hopefully, this "question and answer" page will address what we were unable to cover in this book. You can write us at francis@inchristsimage.org.

I realize that what I have presented here is quite inadequate. However, let's unite in prayer, trusting God that, in His grace, He will raise up others who will join this effort to end church splits and divisions. Together, let's take faith that, within our generation, we will see Christ's church united and God's people healed of this curse of division and splits.

PART ONE:

THE SIN OF DIVISION AND SPLITS

"And there was war in heaven . . . "
—Revelation 12:7

CHAPTER ONE

THE GREAT DIVISION

Lucifer's terrible crime was not only that he rebelled against God, as evil as that was. Worse, through slander against God and deception, he stole away a third of the angels as well. Though banished to hell, Lucifer's war against the Almighty continues. Indeed, every time he divides another church, part of his goal is to strike again the heart of God.

I f you have ever been through a church split, you are all too familiar with the terrible churning of emotions and the inconsolable distress that accompanies this descent into hell. If you are unfamiliar with the experience, expect that large factions of otherwise nice Christians will be pitted against one another. They will participate in slander, anger, deception, fear, bitterness, hatred, gossip, unforgiveness, strife, rebellion and pride.

Any of these attitudes, isolated in a single individual, would be recognized and exposed as sin. However, when they occur en masse in a church split, they are somehow considered righteous. Anger is redefined as "fighting for a principle." Slander and gossip now enlist as allies "in search of the truth."

The epicenter of the split may have been localized in a single church, but the shockwaves are felt across the area-wide body of Christ. News of the conflict is communicated in whispered tones, like when hearing of a family member who has a serious cancer. And it is a cancer—a split is a malignant life system, a false growth that is empowered by anger, pride and ambition instead of the meekness and patience of Christ.

Citywide church leaders shake their heads and sigh. Even if they barely knew the troubled church, they suffer sympathy pains. They are concerned. Those who have experienced the heartache of their own split also shudder, as they remember the still unresolved conflict they carry regarding those who divided their church. Still other pastors become restless and more guarded over their flocks, wary lest the spirit of strife infiltrate their churches as well.

Additionally, the evangelists of the city know that, at least for a season, it will be harder to win the lost. Indeed, as rumors and details of the split reach the ears of the unsaved, the pettiness and politics that accompany a split remind the unbelieving world of why they are keeping their distance from church.

I have traveled throughout most of the Christian world speaking to pastors and church leaders. It is my experience that, while divisions are found everywhere, splits are more frequent and often more mean-spirited in America. Is it our fierce love of independence and freedom? Or is it because of our more aggressive cultural nature? Regardless, American splits tend to have the least civility.

The reasons for church splits are many. Divisions may originate from confusion concerning church governments. To whom has God really given final authority in any given congregation? Sometimes, the root of conflict is simply misguided ambition in one or more associate leaders. And, of course, there is always the issue of spiritual warfare. Often, just as a church begins an upward swing in attendance or spiritual growth, demonically manipulated strife emerges. So, we must ask ourselves: When we see a serious division in a church, are we really looking at the work of the same kind of spirit that manipulated Absalom, Korah or Jezebel?

Perhaps splits involve some combination of all of the above. Yet, regardless of the unique source of each division, Jesus warned that when our house is divided, it "shall not stand" (Matt 12:25). Clearly, when a division strikes a church, its impact is felt throughout the community. It is a war in which the devil is the only one who wins.

HEARTACHE IN HEAVEN

We may think the Lord is personally unfamiliar with the pain of a church split. He is not. In fact, pastors can take some comfort that God Himself, even in all His perfections, suffered a type of split. You may recall that, before the creation of man, heaven endured a time of great rebellion, a "split," if you will.

In those days Satan was known as Lucifer or "Hillel Ben Shahar" in the Hebrew language. The name *Hillel* came from the root word, *Hallel,* which means "to praise, worship, adore"; *Ben Shahar* meant "son of the dawn." The implication is that Lucifer was the chief worship leader at the dawn of creation. Endowed with the gifts of leadership and creativity in music, his position was not enough for him. Fueled by jealousy and ambition, Lucifer led a third of the angels to rebel against the authority of God.

Consider the cunning of Lucifer, our ancient foe. He was able to actually convince angels, who were gazing upon the resplendent glory of God, that they could win a war against their Creator! In privileged awe they had seen galaxies emerge from the mouth of God. Yet somehow they came to believe that, under Lucifer's leadership, they could defeat the Almighty.

They knew God was fully cognizant of their every thought, yet they believed they could outthink Him. Through stealth, slander and seduction, Lucifer engendered discontentment among the angels so that the very pleasures of heaven could not satisfy them. He then lured them from the unimaginable splendor of God's presence, convincing them the unfathomable outer darkness was more suited for their cause. Yes, consider the deceptive powers of our ancient foe and wonder not that he could separate good friends in a church split here on earth.

How long the rebellion in heaven lasted, we do not know. Or what deception Lucifer spun, it is not written. The Bible only grants fleeting reflections into that horrible, cataclysmic divide. Still, one wonders: Did the Lord remain unaffected by the strife? Was the Heavenly Father perfectly aloof from the pain of separation or did He suffer heartache when those whom He gave the gift of life rebelled against Him? Remember, God watched the great lie spread, infecting one angel after another, until a full third joined in the insurrection. Was this division the first great pain in the heart of God?

Beloved, consider also with trembling fear: Until this ancient split, to our knowledge, hell did not exist. Hell became a reality as a consequence of division.

In subsequent chapters we will look at some of the causes as well as some cures for divisions and splits. We will discuss kingdom protocols and expose how the enemy can manipulate our religious ambitions. We will also look at healing a wounded church and restoring the broken pastor. We will even examine the rare times when God allows a split. For now, it is enough that we acknowledge division and splits are serious sins. They remind God of when hell began.

Lord, forgive us for tolerating this terrible sin. Master, we know that our division is a blight upon Your people. Cleanse us of the effects of division and empower each of us with grace to bring unity to Your church. In Jesus' name. Amen.

— CHAPTER TWO —

THE ISSUE IS NOT THE ISSUE

*The Father has decreed Christ's church shall be united.
Indeed, His Son has purchased it and the Holy Spirit is here
to establish it. The battle you are facing is a distraction; the
real issue is to maintain the oneness of Christ.*

I n the last chapter, we marveled that heaven itself endured
a time of strife, a war during which Lucifer challenged the
authority and leadership of God. The Scriptures reveal
that a third of the angels succumbed to the persuasion of
Lucifer's spell (see Rev 12). Ancient traditions say that Lucifer,
together with Michael, Uriel and Gabriel, was originally one of
the great archangels (2 Esdras 4). We cannot verify it, but we
can imagine that the angels who fell were those who, in the
authority structure of heaven, were under Lucifer.

We do not know what lie was so intoxicating that Satan
could lure angels from heaven; what we do know, however, was
that hell was created for those who believed the devil's lie (Matt

25:41). Yet, although Lucifer and his hosts were banished to "pits of darkness" (2 Peter 2:4), their war with heaven did not end. Starting with Adam and Eve, the devil continued his war against God. Indeed, the strife Christians experience today, in a real way, is a continuation of the great primeval conflict.

Recall also that, when Lucifer lured the angels from God, he spoke such vile slander that glorious angels soon became hardened demons. While the Father knew beforehand of Lucifer's plans and rebellion, I cannot imagine the fall of the angels did not grieve the Lord's heart. Yes, and our divisions, engendered by Satan, further strike against the heart of God.

ONE WHO DIVIDES

One truth that will help us defeat the enemy is knowing that, when a church is suffering the heartbreak of division, what seem to be the issues are often not the issue at all. Indeed, when Lucifer fell, from heaven's standpoint, he no longer retained the name Lucifer, but instead was called "Satan" or the "devil." The meaning of these two names gives us a view into the nature of what we are fighting during a split.

Satan means "one who opposes" or "adversary." What power strengthens the confrontational attitude of those in opposition to the established church authority? What evil emboldens those who now disregard love, church order and civility to obtain their desires? The power reinforcing the inability to reconcile is satanic, and it can wedge itself between those in dissent and those in leadership. All sides must beware. Satan will fiercely oppose the idea of healing and reconciliation.

Let us also look at the name *devil,* which means "slanderer." To slander means more than "to speak evil of one to another." Speaking literally, it means *"one who puts himself or some thing between two in order to divide them."*

Satan's goal is not just to speak evil, it is to put something between people in order to divide them. This dividing work destroys friendships, marriages and churches. He will exaggerate what seems wrong in one person and twist the remarks of the other person's reaction. He will frustrate our attempts to compromise and will repeatedly divide Christians with new issues.

It is a mark of a church under demonic attack that the criticisms of the divisive group never let up: settle one issue and three more erupt. When Satan manipulates a splinter group within a church, the issues that inflame them are actually unsatisfiable. The pastor's answers do not satisfy nor are attempts to compromise or find balance usually effective.

The issues rising between opposing camps are a smoke screen used by Satan to divide and conquer a church. They seem real enough, but when an issue becomes more central to our relationship than humility, love and faith, that issue is really a wedge sent to divide.

You see, the issue is not the color of the new carpet or the style of praise and worship or how long the sermon should be; the real issue is, in spite of our differences, will we defend the unity of Christ within the fellowship?

CHRIST, THE UNIFYING FACTOR

Just as the devil's goal is to put himself or some thing between people to divide them, so Christ puts Himself among us in order to heal us and bring unity. While He instructs us to honor our leaders within a church, He also tells us to prefer one another and submit to one another in holy fear. As we seek His forgiveness for our sins, He reminds us that, to receive His forgiveness, we must also forgive others (see Matt 6 & 18). And again, He decrees that if we are at the altar and there remember someone has something against us, we are to leave our offering and seek to be reconciled (see Matt 5:23–24).

Additionally, the Lord puts His Spirit and His cross between us, reminding us that our issues are not the issue: *He is!* Like Jonathan spoke in covenant with David, "May the LORD be between you and me . . . forever" (1 Sam 20:42 NKJV). God places His Son between us, not issues. The only other issue we might ponder is, how can we, in this potential conflict, become examples to others of God's redemptive grace?

IF YOU ARE IN A SPLIT

When division strikes a church, there are three primary groups that are usually involved. The first group consists of those who have initiated the division. They have issues with the leader or the pastoral team. They are discontent with the status quo and desire significant changes in the fellowship. The second group is the current senior leader and his staff who, though embattled, remain loyal to him or at least supportive of his position as pastor. The third group is usually the largest, comprised of those caught in the middle of the division. These are the innocent sheep who have relationships with their leaders but are also friends with the dissenters. Hearing slander and rumors, they are confused and are unsure of what to believe or who to follow.

The dissenting group may use apparently spiritual issues to empower their cause: "We just want more of God." Or, "We want more freedom to grow." Such arguments seem both innocent and legitimate until we remember that anyone can seek God and enjoy more of Him at any time; there is no need to divide the church to have more of God's presence, especially since the division itself will cause God's manifest presence to withdraw!

As the conflict remains unresolved, two groups in the church, each with their own leaders, are rising in opposition. Who do you follow? To discern the true shepherd among you, recall the wisdom of Solomon. When two women came, each claiming a newborn as her own, as a test, Solomon ordered the child to be split in two. The true mother begged that the child remain alive. The false mother, however, agreed to let the baby be split in two. Solomon recognized that the one who loved the child the most, the true mother, would not allow her baby to be divided. Thus, he recognized her parental love and awarded her with her offspring (see 1Kings 3:16–27).

In your church, the true shepherd will be the one who seeks to keep your church together. He will not initiate a split as a solution. He will not kill the baby by dividing it. He will seek, rather, to settle the legitimate issues while maintaining his focus on the higher issue of Christ-centered unity and healing.

Remember, we are not implying that there are not valid issues to discuss with our leaders. Nor are we saying that churches shouldn't become more effective in ministry—indeed, some of the best ideas often come from the congregation! We are only stating that the conflict that divides us is often the enemy's smoke screen. The real issue is this: In spite of conflict, will we maintain meekness, love and unity? Will we, with Christlike integrity, defend the heart of God against Satan's quest to divide us?

Lord, forgive us for allowing divisions and splits to become such deeply ingrained traditions in Christianity. We confess that we are easily manipulated by false issues. Lord, make us instruments of healing. Help us to work with You to unite the church and prepare Your bride. Help us to see the real issue: in all our diversity, will we remain united? In Jesus' Name. Amen.

CHAPTER THREE

When Little Ones Stumble

Nothing so offends the heart of God as when children or new believers are caused to sin.

C learly, one of the most important reasons to avoid a church split, or to open ourselves up to anger and division, is the effect church conflicts have upon our children. The unresolved memory of a painful church split incubates long and silently in the souls of children. Though they outwardly continue in church attendance Sunday after Sunday with their parents, their wounded souls assign a minimal value on the benefits of church in general. When they are old enough, many young people walk away from church forever.

Thus, the most affected victims of church splits are the children. Inevitably, at some point during the conflict, they hear their parents speaking angrily about the pastor or other church members. The children, who really have no part in the conflict, are now forced to take sides. With the parents of their beloved friends on the other side of the division, it is an unbearable injustice to inflict upon children of any age.

Let me reinforce the issue about causing little ones, or new believers, to stumble. To do so, I need to share with you how I came to Christ. My prayer is that God's people would learn the fear of the Lord and that, at all costs, we would avoid causing children to stumble.

The date was November 24, 1970. I was living in a farmhouse in the Blue Ridge Mountains of Virginia with about fourteen other people—all were Christians except one other person and myself. At that time of my life, I wouldn't have called myself a pagan, but nearly all in the home would have. Actually, I considered myself an earnest seeker of God. During the years that the Lord was drawing me to Himself, though I didn't know the Lord personally, I often felt the warm touch of His presence, so much so that I even referred to the interactive, wooing influence of the Holy Spirit as my *invisible friend.*

However, during these pre-Christian years I had also amassed a lot of false information, which I compiled from many religions. So, while sincerely in search of God, I had begun my quest by rejecting the denominational Christianity of my youth and blindly opening myself to Eastern religions and New Age teachers. The result was that I had developed my own private religion.

The farmhouse was heated by wood stoves strategically placed in various rooms throughout the dwelling. One stove was to my immediate right and it heated the dining room where I was sitting. On my left was a long dining room table from which I had pulled my chair to talk to the three novice Christians who were sitting on a couch against the wall. One by one they took turns witnessing to me. However, I not only had deftly defended my views, but my self-made philosophy was beginning to undermine their faith.

"At their essence, all religions are the same," I said, "each in its own way calls us to good works." I then used what I thought was a clever play on words: "In Hinduism, there exists the 'atman' or 'world soul' which is the beginning of all souls; in science, the 'atom' sits at life's beginning; in Christianity, we all come from 'Adam.' So, it doesn't matter whether we refer to atman, atom or Adam; whether we are Christian or followers of Krishna—they all even sound the same."

I spoke confidently. Not only had my words silenced these new believers, I bewildered them. I "counter-witnessed" and won. The result was that their faith was shaken while my philosophy remained secure. The discussion was over and, with only an awkward silence filling the room, I turned and scooted my chair back to its spot at the head of the table. There, resting on the place setting, was a large, "red-letter" Bible; it was opened to the eighteenth chapter of the book of Matthew. Someone earlier had left it at the table.

You should understand that, along with the "holy books" I read from other religions, I also esteemed the Bible. It was a book through which God spoke. Now, something strange was happening to me. I wasn't reading this Bible on the table; it was "reading" me. My attention had been captured by the blood red words of the sixth verse:

> Whoever causes one of these little ones who believe in Me to stumble, it is better for him that a heavy millstone be hung around his neck, and that he be drowned in the depth of the sea. —Matthew 18:6

Up to that moment, I had been thinking fairly well of myself. In fact, I thought I had just "enlightened" three naive young Christians, helping them to not be so narrow-minded. Suddenly, the words of this verse, like lightning, bolted into my eyes and shot straight into the darkness of my heart. Throughout my entire being I was instantly aware that the God of these Christians was very angry with me. I had just done what this verse warned against: I caused His little ones to stumble!

All my philosophers, those supposedly great sages whose books I devoured, had left their ideas to mankind and then departed; *but Jesus Christ was actually with these young Christians!* He was not a mere religion. He was their living Shepherd and very capable Savior—and He was protecting them from me!

My *invisible friend* was, suddenly, no longer friendly! He was, in fact, aggressively hostile. The impact of His anger was like a punch to my chest. It knocked the breath from my lungs. The color drained from my face. My palms sweat.

I felt physically wounded!

I may have just won the debate, but I was rapidly, unconditionally, losing the war. I couldn't talk, except to manage a frail "I'm sorry" as I stumbled toward the bathroom, which was the only place in the crowded farmhouse where I could be alone.

"Lord, please forgive me. I'll never do that again," I said repeatedly as I sat trembling on the bathroom floor. Suddenly, though, I had a revelation: Just as the ancient sages trained and mentored their followers, since Jesus Christ was truly alive, perhaps He would accept me as His disciple. Obviously, though invisible, He had no problem communicating with me! In His mercy, the Lord was building a bridge into my thought processes so He could personally free me from my deception.

Incredibly, though, I still did not "officially" become a Christian—that would happen two days later, on Thanksgiving night. But now, in a frightening way, I knew Jesus was real. I also knew, eternally and indelibly, that the way to quickly rouse His anger was to cause a new believer to stumble.

THE HOLY FEAR OF GOD

We have an erroneous idea that God is a little like Santa Claus: always jovial, kind, and busy working on a new present for us. However, there are certain things the Almighty abhors—things which activate His wrath.

What kind of life do you think awaits the man who is doing what God hates? The book of Proverbs lists seven attitudes that will surely and quickly invoke God's wrath; the worst thing He hates, He mentions last:

> There are six things which the LORD hates, yes, seven which are an abomination to Him: Haughty eyes, a lying tongue, and hands that shed innocent blood, a heart that devises wicked plans, feet that run rapidly to evil, a false witness who utters lies, and one who spreads strife among brothers.　　　　　　　　—Proverbs 6:16–19

Each of these sins manifest in varying degrees during a church split, the worst being those who spread strife among brothers. God hates it for many reasons, but the most terrible thing it does is cause little ones to stumble.

If we are involved in spreading strife, we are awakening God's wrath. You see, a church is not a "religious museum" where ancient artifacts are revered; it is a community united by a common relationship with Christ and, through Christ, thereby united with one another. From heaven's view, God dwells in the harmony of our common relationship with Him.

God defines eternal life by the condition of our relationships. Yet, in a church split, relationships are brutalized and many people stumble. Old friends become new enemies. People who once prayed for each other now prey on each other. Worse, new believers stumble badly, wondering how mature, spiritual leaders could divide over such inconsequential issues usually accompanying church divisions. Meanwhile, because of such pettiness, "pre-believers," those close to coming to Christ, recognize this cannot possibly be right, and they walk away from God.

Instead of rivers of living water flowing from the innermost being of church fellowship, a deep, sickening feeling churns in the pit of every stomach. The whole church feels it. This is so serious, so opposite the essence of God's kingdom. Jesus tells us that, if we are at the altar and there remember someone has something against us, we are commanded to leave our offering and be reconciled with our brother (Matt 5:24). He is saying, in effect: "Your religious church service isn't as important to Me as your relationship with your estranged brother."

LET US WIN SOULS, NOT OFFEND THEM!

Jesus said, " 'Woe to that man through whom the stumbling block comes!' " (Matt 18:7) Dear ones, listen: If you are following a man willing to split a church to fulfill a ministry call, beware. How can one who willingly tears apart relationships be genuinely concerned about relationships? How can anyone who is willing to cause little ones to stumble be walking toward the blessing and approval of Jesus Christ?

I have told you the story of how I came to Christ, and the warning the Lord gave me. Beloved friend, if you desire to start a church, find ways that do not divide your present church nor cause people to stumble. God has protocols that must be followed. If what we are planning has caused division, and children and new believers are stumbling, then we are absolutely going in the wrong direction.

Leaders, in order to safeguard our churches from division, we must have a church growth strategy that creates positive, redemptive opportunities for people to be released in ministry functions. This may be as simple as a recommended Bible college or as sophisticated as a broad church planting strategy. Let us develop clear, positive alternatives so church splits do not become options. While we must protect the flock, let us not become possessive. God gives us authority to spiritually liberate His people and equip them for ministry. Let's do our part to find ways to train and release maturing Christians.

I have never recovered from that first frightening encounter with God. It abides as a living, holy fear within me. I am concerned for new believers. I know that the Lord Himself will personally turn hostile for the sake of His sheep, and I cannot bear the thought of rousing God's anger against me. So, in defense of the Lord's people and in service to the Lord's heart, I repeat to you the words of the Lord Jesus Christ:

Whoever causes one of these little ones who believe in Me to stumble, it is better for him that a heavy millstone be hung around his neck, and that he be drowned in the depth of the sea.   —Matthew 18:6

Lord Jesus, forgive me for thinking my needs were more important than Yours and the needs of children. Master, You taught that children are the most important people in Your kingdom. Father, forgive me for causing them to stumble. In Jesus' name. Amen.

PART TWO:

HOW STRIFE
BEGINS

*"For lack of wood the fire goes out,
and where there is no whisperer, contention
quiets down. Like charcoal to hot embers
and wood to fire,
so is a contentious man to kindle strife."*
—Proverbs 26:20–21

CHAPTER FOUR

LUCIFER'S NATURE: AMBITION

No virtue manifests in our lives without Satan awakening a corresponding vice: Traveling with obedience is pride, and just behind faith walks presumption. Yes, and walking in the shadow of godly vision, ambition follows.

There are perhaps many sources of strife that lead to divisions and splits, but none are more subtle nor powerful than religious ambition. This is especially so when a subordinate leader begins to imagine God has called them to take the place of a senior leader or department head.

As we again reflect back to the first great division, through the prophet Isaiah, the Holy Spirit gives us insight into the motive of Lucifer's rebellion against divine authority: selfish ambition. This revelation of Lucifer's ambition manifests succinctly through the voice of the Babylonian king mentioned in Isaiah 14 (actually identified as "Lucifer" in the King James

Bible). Listen to the edict of God against the unholy objectives of the prince of darkness:

> How you are fallen from heaven, O Lucifer, son of the morning! How you are cut down to the ground, you who weakened the nations! For you have said in your heart: "I will ascend into heaven; I will exalt my throne above the stars of God; I will also sit on the mount of the congregation on the farthest sides of the north; I will ascend above the heights of the clouds; I will be like the Most High."   —Isaiah 14:12–14 NKJV

A number of Bible commentators agree that this quote, though ascribed to a man, actually embodies Lucifer's unrestrained lust for preeminence and position. Five times the focus of Lucifer's pride speaks through the king's great ambition: "I will," until he states plainly his unholy quest to supplant God as the supreme being worshiped on planet earth.

Lucifer not only desires to be like God, but he seeks to "ascend to heaven" and establish his throne above the stars of God, which is where the Almighty sits! The Revelation of John confirms this goal repeatedly throughout the book: Satan seeks to be worshiped. He seeks the place of God in heaven and he seeks the place of God in us.

This is vital for our discernment: *Satan is primarily a religious spirit.* He does not want to destroy the world; he wants to rule it. He led a third of the angels against God's authority in heaven, and he manipulates religious ambition in subordinate leaders to usurp God's delegated authority in His church on earth.

Of course, Lucifer's involvement in the religion of man is widespread and multifaceted, but nothing he does is more subtle or diabolical than when he deceives good Christians to turn against their own church leaders. Astutely, Jesus warned that a "house divided against itself shall not stand" (Matt 12:25).

Listen well, it is right to aspire to the office of an overseer; it is wrong to be ambitious for the office of *your* overseer. It is honorable to desire a church to serve as shepherd; it is hellish to engender discontent against the leader of your current church so you can take his place.

Because a subordinate leader cannot simply take the place of the senior leader through physical force, he must work covertly. He has to make himself appear righteous and find ways to make the senior leader appear unrighteous, or at least not as righteous or wise as the subordinate postures himself to be. The one in rebellion always has an issue; there is always something not right—and if he were in charge, he would do all things better. Reasonable communication or compromise on problems which are not serious sin issues will never remedy the conflict, because the subordinate does not want compromise; he desires control. As Lucifer seeks to take the place of God, so the subordinate covets the pastor's position.

Whenever we seek to take the place of another whom God has placed in authority, we are conforming ourselves to the image of Lucifer, not Christ.

GODLY VISION, FLESHLY MOTIVES

The deception surrounding ambition is especially powerful when someone actually has a vision from God but seeks to fulfill it in the flesh. Early in my spiritual journey, the Lord gave me a vision about my future. It was an exciting promise, alive with the glory and power of God, bursting with hope to reach nations for Christ. However, other than focusing me on the presence of the Lord, the vision came without any specifics as to when or how it would be fulfilled.

In those days, I thought the Lord's promise was the same as His command, something I had to fulfill in whatever way I could. Indeed, because of my spiritual immaturity, I could find no reason why the Lord's promise should not be fulfilled quickly. (When one is immature, he does not realize he is immature, because he is immature.)

According to my imagination, it would be easy for God to fulfill His promise, and I had a preponderance of ideas to help Him. Young as I was spiritually, I was simply unfamiliar with the Holy Spirit's work of preparation: the call to die to self, the seasons of learning patience and maintaining vision through testing—all of which needed to occur before the vision from the Almighty would draw near to fulfillment.

A true word from God will test you before it fulfills you. Consider Joseph. The Scripture says, "Until the time that his word came to pass, the word of the LORD tested him" (Ps 105:19). The longer my spiritual fulfillment delayed, the more my character was being forced to change. With great passion I wanted my destiny to unfold; I just did not want God's discipline. With unrelenting hope, I desired the crown God set before me; I just didn't see the cross that stood between the Father's initial promise and my spiritual fulfillment.

I have come to believe that it is probably impossible to gain spiritual advancement without ambition rising within us. In and of itself, I don't even think ambition is blatantly wrong as long as our zeal is guarded by humility and submission. To have ambition, yet be able to wait, trust God, and put others first means the Holy Spirit rules our lives, and thus transforms ambition into patient obedience. It is when ambition and pride unite that we become spiritually dangerous.

But let me say, even if our motives are not perfect, we need to persist with our destiny. Don't become so introspective that you stop walking forward. There are many times, especially in our early years, when we must persevere in spite of our pride and fleshly motives. Ask God to correct you as you move forward; don't be afraid to take faith and step out. However, let us be aware of those times when our zeal is creating strife and confusion around us. For when we are causing strife, we are moving away from our destiny, not toward it.

Ambition might arise as a consequence of faith, but it is not faith. Ambition is the attempt of the flesh to fulfill the promise of the Spirit. In my inner person, I considered my ambition to be a virtue; I was actually proud of it. Abraham had it when, in his impatience, it caused him and Hagar to produce Ishmael. Ultimately, the Lord said of Ishmael, "He will be a wild donkey of a man, his hand will be against everyone, and everyone's hand will be against him" (Gen 16:12). In other words, he would be a constant source of strife. Ambition, when driving us to move ahead of the Lord's timing, will almost always produce strife in those around us.

True faith, however, rests in God's integrity and faithfulness. A person of faith can entrust his calling and gifts to the timing and wisdom of God. Thus, true faith rests in God, even when what is promised is not yet seen. It does not strive, it trusts. Abraham's faith outgrew his ambition because he learned to trust that the Lord was faithful (see Heb 10:23). He became "fully assured that what [God] had promised, He was able also to perform" (Rom 4:21).

The ambitious soul, however, fails to trust God for the timing and opening of appropriate doors; it spawns impatience and striving to fulfill one's destiny. Ambition tries to create doors where none exist.

The Bible tells us plainly that none of those whom God used were able to avoid an extended time of preparation. God's call and His timing are the work of His hands. Our task is to remain faithful to the place He has us in and to maintain integrity in support of others.

Ambition creates strife, in part, because it is rooted in fear. This fear brings striving and jealousy into the Christian's soul, especially as others occupy positions we deem necessary for our fulfillment. Because we do not truly know the Lord in the way of patience and trust, the voice we most often obey is not God's, but the urgency of our own ambition.

Consequently, James tells us, "Where jealousy and selfish ambition exist," there will inevitably emerge "disorder and every evil thing" (James 3:16). Disorder comes as people violate proper protocols for spiritual advancement and begin to criticize those in a position over or alongside them. Disorder opens the door for "every evil thing" to enter, as attention is drawn away from the pastor's God-appointed responsibilities and given to lengthy, usually fruitless, meetings spent trying to remedy strife.

Ambition is obsessed with fulfillment. When rebuked, though it puts on the face of the penitent; it grows angrier because of the new delay. There is only one remedy for religious ambition: it must die.

The Path to Leadership

If you are a subordinate leader and desire your own church, do not find fault with your current leader as a means of seeking advancement. The answer to your success is unveiled in Psalm 37. Here David revealed the attitude that ultimately promoted him to kingship. Remember, David was submitted to King Saul, an unjust king driven by fits of madness. Still, David wrote,

> Trust in the LORD, and do good; dwell in the land and cultivate faithfulness. Delight yourself in the LORD; and He will give you the desires of your heart. Commit your way to the LORD, trust also in Him, and He will do it. And He will bring forth your righteousness as the light, and your judgment as the noonday. Rest in the LORD and wait patiently for Him; do not fret because of him who prospers in his way, because of the man who carries out wicked schemes. Cease from anger, and forsake wrath; do not fret, it leads only to evildoing.
>
> —Psalm 37:3–8

Even though in my earlier years I wrestled with my own ambitions of spiritual fulfillment, I never sought the place of another leader. I learned to trust in the Lord and do good. I saw that fretting over what was wrong in those around me only led to evil doing. Let us therefore, cease from anger and forsake wrath. Let us delight ourselves in the Lord and He will give us the desires of our hearts at the proper time.

Lord Jesus, forgive me for my selfish motives and unbroken will. I confess there have been times when my pride and ambition have generated strife. I have been so blind to this. Help me to serve You with my whole heart and let You promote me at the proper time. For Your glory, I pray. Amen.

CHAPTER FIVE

THREE SPIRITUAL ENEMIES OF UNITY

It is important to realize that, while we are dealing with the weakness of flesh and blood, our true fight is not against people, but "spiritual forces of wickedness" (Eph 6:12).

J ust as we stated that the issue is not the issue, so the apparent enemy is not the real enemy. We are not fighting people, but the spirits that manipulate immature or sinful attitudes of heart in people. These spirits seek to gain access to our churches and families; they must be discerned. Religious ambition in the human heart is just the entry point for the enemies we are truly fighting: the spirits of division and strife.

The nature and goal of these spirits are the same: to inspire someone to seek in an ungodly way another person's position of authority, thus causing division. This is the ancient battle transported to modern times with flesh and blood role players. Recall Jude's warning,

And angels who did not keep their own domain, but abandoned their proper abode, He has kept in eternal bonds under darkness for the judgment of the great day.
—Jude 1:6

When we unethically abandon our "proper abode" and seek the role of another, we are embracing the very sin Lucifer and his angels committed. Just as their sin led to hell, so their manipulation of earthly ambitions extends hell into the lives of men and women on earth.

While they share the same goal of creating division, their approaches to separating people are unique. The Old Testament provides three examples of individuals who usurped authority and divided the people of God: Korah, Absalom and Jezebel. Although these individuals were real people with historic lives, for the sake of classification we will assign their names to the spirits that manipulated them. When we discuss these enemies, we are looking through the human personality at the spirit which seeks to find modern counterparts, again bringing strife between God's people.

KORAH: THE LEADER WHO WANTS IT ALL

The New Testament writer Jude mentions specifically the "rebellion of Korah" (Jude 1:11). Korah was a leader in ancient Israel; he was equal to Aaron in authority and was a cousin to both Moses and Aaron. Through his influence, he was able to seduce 250 of Israel's princes to join him in a rebellion against Moses.

The worst divisions among God's people are those which are led by subordinate leaders who have acquired a large following. Matthew Henry's Commentary says of Korah and the other leaders in rebellion: "Note, the pride, ambition, and emulation, of great men, have always been the occasion of a great deal of mischief both in churches and states . . . The fame and renown which they had did not content them; they were high, but would be higher, and thus the famous men became infamous."

Although, Matthew Henry is speaking of Korah, clearly he could be describing Lucifer himself or any subordinate leader who has tasted of success, is discontent they do not have more power, and envious of those above them. Beware when we desire the position of our leaders.

Listen to Korah's accusation against Moses and Aaron: "You take too much upon yourselves . . . Why then do you exalt yourselves above the assembly of the LORD?" (Num 16:3 NKJV) While it is Korah who is in rebellion, he charges that *Moses* is rebelling against God and is domineering in his leadership. It is Korah who is seeking to exalt himself, yet he accuses Moses and Aaron of exalting themselves "above the assembly."

As a means of spiritual discernment, listen carefully to the one who accuses your pastoral leadership. Even before you examine your pastor, examine his accuser. For you will often see in him the very flaws he says are in the pastor.

As a further argument, Korah states that "all Israel is holy and the Lord is among them." The implication is that Korah is actually the one most concerned for the people, that Moses' task is complete, and it is time for new leadership to be appointed.

Of course, at this time all Israel was not holy nor was the assignment of Moses complete. But these things were said to reinforce the accusation that Moses was a domineering personality who was primarily seeking to maintain control of Israel.

Friends, there are times when a senior leader may truly be overly controlling, and we will soon discuss that. But there is another time when our wrong attitude toward authority will cause us to misjudge a leader as "controlling" when he is, in fact, simply fulfilling his God-given spiritual responsibility. God had appointed Moses as Israel's leader. God chose him on the basis of his meekness, a trait that was little esteemed by those who sought to remove him from leadership. Remember: to usurp the authority that God has installed is to sin against the Lord Himself.

Moses responded to Korah,

> Hear now, you sons of Levi, is it not enough for you that the God of Israel has separated you from the rest of the congregation of Israel, to bring you near to Himself, to do the service of the tabernacle of the LORD, and to stand before the congregation to minister to them; and that He has brought you near, Korah, and all your brothers, sons of Levi, with you? And are you seeking for the priesthood also?   —Numbers 16:8–10

Moses exposes the sin of envy and ambition in Korah's heart. He asks, "Is it not enough for you" that you already have a position set apart to God? Ambition walks upon two legs: envy and pride. Whenever we covet the position God has assigned to another, we are attracting the Lord's anger to ourselves. Indeed, the story of Korah's rebellion concludes with the ground swallowing Korah and those in rebellion with him.

It is noteworthy that both Korah and Jethro, Moses' father-in-law, approached Moses with a similar statement. Korah was confrontational and filled with ambition and rebellion; Jethro was humble and filled with concern. When Jethro saw all that Moses was doing, he said, "What is this thing that you are doing for the people? Why do you alone sit as judge and all the people stand about you from morning until evening?" (Exod 18:14).

To express concern to a leader in a humble manner is an asset to any church; to confront the leader out of pride and ambition, as did Korah, is to expose yourself to the wrath of God. Under Jethro's counsel, Israel prospered. Never be afraid to submit your observations to leaders. Give your advice; then let them administrate it as they see fit.

An interesting side note was that the sons of Korah did not die in their father's rebellion. They chose, instead, to be submissive to Moses and Aaron. In time, the sons of Korah held a place of great honor in David's day, actually writing a number of the Psalms, which we study today as sacred Scriptures.

To be free from the influences of the Korah spirit, we must be content to wholeheartedly serve God where He has currently placed us. A time may come when a new order or new assignment comes to us from the Holy Spirit, but until then the Lord will not require us to challenge the authority of those over us nor divide the church so we can fulfill our religious ambitions.

THE ABSALOM SPIRIT

Nelson's Bible Dictionary tells us that "Absalom was the third son by Maacah, the daughter of the king of Geshur (2 Sam 3:3; 1 Chron 3:2). Of royal descent on both sides, Absalom was a potential heir to the throne. Attractive in appearance and charming in manners, he was also a popular prince with the people and a favorite of his father."

However, although a favorite of his father and the people, Absalom suffered the injustice of his half sister's rape by Amnon, another of David's sons. In retaliation, Absalom had Amnon murdered by his servants. Fearing the wrath of his father for the murder of Amnon, he fled to Geshur, where he lived in exile for three years. Finally, under pressure from his leaders, David reluctantly sent for Absalom, yet shunned him when he returned. The long delay and his father's indifference produced a bitterness in Absalom toward the king, which ripened into a plan to steal his father's throne:

> Absalom used to rise early and stand beside the way to the gate; and it happened that when any man had a suit to come to the king for judgment, Absalom would call to him and say, "From what city are you?" And he would say, "Your servant is from one of the tribes of Israel."

> Then Absalom would say to him, "See, your claims are good and right, but no man listens to you on the part of

the king." Moreover, Absalom would say, "Oh that one would appoint me judge in the land, then every man who has any suit or cause could come to me, and I would give him justice." And it happened that when a man came near to prostrate himself before him, he would put out his hand and take hold of him and kiss him. And in this manner Absalom dealt with all Israel who came to the king for judgment; so Absalom stole away the hearts of the men of Israel.   —2 Samuel 15:2–6

Just as Korah sought Moses' place, and Lucifer before him sought the place of God, so Prince Absalom sought the throne of King David. At first, however, Absalom was not openly confrontational of David, nor did he seek to challenge the king's authority. Rather, Absalom used his charm and subtle criticisms of the king to steal away the hearts of men.

Again, the New Testament writer Jude gives us an insight into this manipulating spirit as it manifests today through people:

These are grumblers, finding fault, following after their own lusts; they speak arrogantly, flattering people for the sake of gaining an advantage . . . These are the ones who cause divisions, worldly-minded, devoid of the Spirit.
                    —Jude 1:16,19

Absalom found fault with David and engendered grumbling in the people of Israel, while winning the hearts of the people with flattery and charm. Jude said, "These are the ones who cause divisions." The plan of the Absalom spirit is simple: Grumble about the way things are not getting done, find fault with the leader, and arrogantly project the image that, if you were in charge, all would be well. Then, to capture the hearts of the people, flatter them and bring them into your camp. Paul also warned about those whom he called "wolves," who "will arise, speaking perverse things, to draw away the disciples after them" (Acts 20:29–30).

To speak "perverse things" means we have twisted or distorted the truth. Beware when someone comes along complaining about the way things are done, speaking evil of the church leader and promoting himself as an answer to these problems. You are probably listening to a wolf in the flock of God. Yet, even in this situation, speak with this person directly and expose his error. Perhaps the Lord will change his heart.

What if the suspicions raised against the senior leader seem to be true? Before you talk to anyone in the congregation, go to the leader himself according to Matthew 18. Go in meekness, entreating him "as a father" (1 Tim 5:1). Hear his side. If he is guilty of serious sin and remains unrepentant, bring with you two or three others. If he continues in sin, public exposure of his error is the final remedy (see Matt 18:15–17). But before you do that, your group should approach other church leaders in the city, or the denomination's district supervisor. Let them administrate the proper discipline.

At the same time, you must be certain he is in serious sin. It is not enough to just "sense" that there is "something wrong under the surface." You must have facts. If his primary "sin" is that he does not feel comfortable going along with the current trend in American Christianity, this is not sin. If you feel you must see certain spiritual manifestations in church, go somewhere where the things you seek are occurring, but do not divide your church, nor speak things to draw disciples after yourself. If you dream of being the leader of the church and are using spiritual phenomena to justify building a constituency, you are walking in the footsteps of Absalom, not Christ.

To free yourself from the influences of the Absalom spirit, repent of pride and refrain from using flattery to gain an advantage among the people. Instead of manipulating the unmet needs of the church to gain a following, submit yourself and your talents to the church leaders. Ask them how you can help. Don't exploit the needs; help meet them. And when you have been used by the Lord, point people to Christ, securing them in the care of the church leaders.

(For further insight on the nature of Absalom, read *A Tale of Three Kings* by Gene Edwards.)

THE JEZEBEL SPIRIT

In the Old Testament, Jezebel was a queen who fought against authority, whether that authority was resident in the spiritual leaders (the prophets) or the secular leader (the king). In the New Testament, Jesus mentions this spirit again, this time manifest as a prophetess in the church in Thyatira. In both settings, this spirit desires to neutralize authority and take control over other people in the church and family.

When the Jezebel spirit attacks church leadership, its ultimate purpose will be to disable the spiritual authority of pastoral leadership. The attack may come in the form of sexual temptation, confusion or prophetic manipulation, but its aim is to supplant the authority in the church.

Thus, Jesus promised that the church that overcomes Jezebel will be granted "authority over the nations" (Rev 2:26). The Jezebel spirit seeks to divide, diminish and then displace the spiritual authority God has given church leaders.

While Korah and Absalom use issues that most often affect men, Jezebel targets women. In the New Testament, Jesus Himself referred to Jezebel as a "woman who calls herself a prophetess" (Rev 2:20). Catch this phrase, "she calls herself." In other words, she is self-appointed and submitted to no one. She uses her prophetic insights and sensitivities to draw a following to herself, again dividing the church from its true base of authority.

If you are a woman who has a propensity to gain control in relationships, the antidote for this influence is true humility. Let the Lord promote you. Stay submissive. Jezebel's quest for control masks a deeper need she has concerning fear. She was probably abused and is afraid of being abused again, so she seeks to control her world using whatever means available. To be healed from the influence of Jezebel, whether it attaches itself to a woman or a man, one must truly learn to trust God.

Because this spirit wars against authority in the church, it will seek to put wedges of division between a pastor and the church intercessors. To counter this potential division, let the senior leader appreciate, communicate and support his intercessors and esteem their contribution; and let the intercessors set their prayer focus to seek the spiritual fulfillment of their pastor's vision.

Without pastors leading in godly authority, a church simply cannot function: confusion, ambition and chaos reign. True spiritual authority is a source of protection; it is a living shelter that covers and nurtures a home or church. Satan seeks to neutralize the leader in that Christian setting, for if he can strike the shepherd, he can scatter the sheep.

And, we need intercessors, for prayer is the frontier of transformation; without intercessors, the church literally would not move forward. However, when an intercessor assumes that their "prophetic witness" is the guiding light of the church, or when they stand apart from the church leader and promote a different vision than what the leadership presents, it is a sign that the spirit of Jezebel may be trying to divide that church.

Indeed, the confusion spreads, as those who present a vision different from the pastor's are usually presenting something that seems godly and reasonable. Yet, the unbending demand that a leader conform to a prophetic witness, or the urgency of its timing, is where the enemy gains access and causes division. So, simply submit your witness to the church leaders and trust God to bring it to pass, if He so chooses, in its proper time.

Intercessors must accept that God has given the church leadership the responsibility to guide the church. The senior leader may draw his vision for the church directly from the Lord or indirectly from his staff. He may find direction from Christian authors, denominational leadership, or some combination of the above. Not the least of his resources, however, are the church intercessors. I personally have been rescued and protected by the faithfulness of humble intercessors who stand in the gap before God on my behalf.

Yet, when an intercessor quietly bypasses the church leadership and seeks to introduce a different vision than that which is currently guiding the church, they are introducing strife and confusion to God's people. As an intercessor myself, let me urge you to simply submit your perceptions and spiritual aspirations to the church leaders. If any change of direction is to come, it should come through their administration.

Intercessors, make your stand to defend the word spoken from the pulpit by the pastor. If his teaching is boring and unimaginative, all the more reason to pray. Take his or her sermon and focus your prayer on that theme during the coming week. There is nothing more powerful than when the teaching in a church and the intercession of that church are in agreement (Zech 12:10; 1 Peter 4:11a). Indeed, small wonder Jezebel seeks to divide the intercessors from the leaders. For when intercessors pray what the pastor preaches, the union of the Spirit and the Word release the creative power of heaven itself.

Lord, help me to see and understand my role in Your kingdom. Master, grant me the meekness of the Holy Spirit, that I might serve without ambition, encourage without manipulation, and intercede without trying to control. Lord, help me to walk in discernment. Free me from any influence other than the ministry of the Holy Spirit Himself. In Jesus' name. Amen.

CHAPTER SIX

ONE OF YOU IS A GOSSIP

"A perverse man spreads strife, and a slanderer separates intimate friends" (Prov 16:28).

J esus made a remarkable statement concerning Judas. He said, " 'Did I Myself not choose you, the twelve, and yet one of you is a devil?' Now He meant Judas the son of Simon Iscariot, for he, one of the twelve, was going to betray Him" (John 6:70–71).

To what was Jesus referring when He identified Judas Iscariot as "a devil"? Was He speaking figuratively or factually? Is Jesus saying that a human being could not only "have" an evil spirit living in his soul, but that a person can actually become a demon?

Some teach that Judas had become so perfectly possessed by Satan that he actually lost his humanity. Before we accept this interpretation, let us remember that, after this fallen apostle delivered Jesus up, he felt such remorse for betraying Christ that he committed suicide. Could a demon feel such remorse for sin? I do not think so.

What I believe Jesus is identifying in Judas Iscariot as a "devil" is something that, today, exists unchecked among many Christians: *slander*. In the New Testament, the Greek word, *diabolos*, which is translated "devil" in this text, is translated impersonally elsewhere as a "false accuser," "slanderer" or "a malicious gossip." In fact, First Timothy 3:11 and Second Timothy 3:3 both translate *diabolos* (Strong's #1228) as "malicious gossip(s)."

In other words, in my opinion, Jesus is not saying "one of you is a devil" in an organic or theological sense, but that one of you is "a slanderer, a malicious gossip." So, while the disciples were almost bragging about their loyalty to Christ, Jesus corrected them, in effect saying, "Yes, I chose you, but even among you there is one who is a malicious gossip, whose words will eventually betray Me to My enemies."

IN THE LAST DAYS

This problem of gossip in the church, Paul tells us, will continue right into the end of the age. Listen carefully to what Paul wrote to Timothy about the last days: "Men will be lovers of self, lovers of money, boastful, arrogant, revilers, disobedient to parents, ungrateful, unholy, unloving, irreconcilable, malicious gossips" (2 Tim 3:2–3). In the midst of this list of great sins of the apostasy, the apostle includes "malicious gossips." This is the exact same word translated "devil" in John 6:70.

Perhaps you know people who always have something negative to say about others, always bringing negative information about people into their conversations. I'm praying that the Holy Spirit will reveal to us how "malicious gossip" is kin to the nature of Satan himself!

The Scriptures say that we will be justified or condemned by our words. Yes, our words, even those spoken in secret with a spouse or friend about others, are used by God to measure our obedience to His will. James writes, "If anyone does not stumble in what he says, he is a perfect man" (James 3:2).

Words have power. Scripture reveals that "Death and life are in the power of the tongue" (Prov. 18:21). Our words, expressed as a confession of faith, brought us into salvation; but words without faith can lead us and others with us into destruction and heartache.

James 3:8 warns, "the tongue . . . is a restless evil . . . full of deadly poison." "The tongue," he says, "is a fire, the very world of iniquity" (v 6). Listen carefully as James reveals a most profound thought. He says that the "tongue . . . sets on fire the course of our life, and is set on fire by hell" (v 6).

Satan gains access to our world, to destroy all that is good and holy in it, through our tongues! The very course of our life, the direction and quality of our earthly existence, is "set on fire by hell" through the words we speak! If we talk negatively about someone or maliciously gossip, the destructive fire of hell itself is released through our words! Lord, help us to understand the power of our words!

I believe God wants to break the power of gossip and negative speaking from the church! We may have a perfect analysis of what is wrong and why it is evil, yet if all we do is talk about it, we have yet to disavow our allegiance to hell. God calls us to be a house of prayer *for* all nations—a spiritual community that is mature, fully capable of seeing what is wrong, but positioning itself to release redemption into the world.

If Paul Visited Your Community

Imagine if the apostle Paul came into a typical American city. Do you know what he might say about our divisions?

Probably what he told the Corinthians, "I am afraid that perhaps when I come . . . there may be strife, jealousy, angry tempers, disputes, slanders, gossip" (2 Cor 12:20).

Does that remind you of any churches anywhere? Strife? Jealousy? Slanders and gossip? How can we approach God with these things existing in us? I believe God desires to give the church a whole new approach. However, we cannot lay hold of the future unless we first let go of the past.

Perhaps you are thinking, "So and so should hear this." Yes, but my hope is that we will start with ourselves. Pastors must stop talking negatively about people; they need to refrain from "leaking" problems with people into their sermons; intercessors must stop negative gossip about the people they should be praying for. If we discuss what is wrong for ten minutes, let us pray for redemption for twenty.

JUDGE NOT

How do you respond to life's imperfections? Do you gossip? When you hear of someone's failure, are you quick to spread the news? If Jesus was looking at the Christians with whom you fellowship, would He say to you what He spoke to His early apostles, that "one of you is a malicious gossip?"

Even if you are not a gossip or slanderer, you must be careful to avoid "fellowship" with gossips. Criticisms incubate. Paul warned that "a little leaven leavens the whole lump." If we walk with the wise, we'll become wise, but if we open our heart to the cynical and critical, we, in fact, become like them. That is why Jesus said we were to "take heed" what we listened to. For whatever we intently focus upon, we absorb in abundance (see Mark 4:24).

Thus, we must not even listen to gossip. When God shows us what is wrong in life, it is so we can pray for redemption, not spread the bad news all over town. Prayer has a very positive focus. People with Christ's love have a spiritual vision that causes them to see beyond the imperfections and limitations of the present world into the potential awaiting in the future—and they pray until what they see comes to pass.

Remember, none of us stands perfectly upright. Every time we judge someone, we position ourselves to be judged as well. Indeed, we each continually lean in the direction of our weakness. Only by the grace of God are we kept from falling. The moment we begin to self-righteously judge or gossip about another for their failings, we lean a little closer toward our own fall.

Let our actions and words be motivated by mercy. If we must discuss the situation or individual, let us harbor no malice or ill will. Let redemption be our guide, not revenge. Let us keep ourselves from becoming those who betray the working of Christ on the earth. Let us keep ourselves from the realm of the malicious gossip.

Lord, purify my lips with fire from Your holy altar. Father, forgive me for my words which have not always been redemptive. Lord, deliver the church from the realm of spreading gossip to the work of spreading grace. Help us to be a house of prayer. In Jesus' name. Amen.

PART THREE:

HEALING THE WOUNDED CHURCH

"I will extol Thee, O Lord,
for Thou hast lifted me up,
and hast not let my enemies rejoice over me.
O LORD my God,
I cried to Thee for help,
and Thou didst heal me."
—Psalm 30:1–2

CHAPTER SEVEN

WHEN
A LEADER SINS

Not many things are more devastating than when someone in authority—someone whom we trusted—betrays our trust and sins. Unless we deal with the effect of this leader's sin, it will always be a source of oppression to us.

Sometimes the motivating force behind a church split has to do with the sins of church leadership. Now, I am not referring to minor offenses or flaws, but sins that are either sexual in nature or a violation of community laws that could lead to incarceration.

Scriptures warn, "Strike the Shepherd that the sheep may be scattered; and I will turn My hand against the little ones" (Zech 13:7). This Scripture in Zechariah refers, of course, to Jesus Christ. He did not sin, but was slandered as though He had. Either way, the effect was the same: a scattering of the little ones.

Satan knows that when the shepherd of a flock is struck, "little ones" are scattered. Thus, there will almost always be more spiritual warfare against a leader than that which typically comes directly against the church. Indeed, much of the warfare against a church is a direct result of the battle against its leader or leadership.

However, sometimes leaders do fall. Men and women alike can fail to gauge the cunning of the enemy and, like anyone, become entrapped in serious sin. When such sin is finally exposed, it has a devastating effect upon a church, so much so that people leave en masse. This kind of split is not caused by the ambition of those who leave, but the failing of one in leadership. For both those who leave and those who remain, a cleansing is necessary in order to guide the sheep back into the blessedness of God's presence.

Transferred Guilt

When church leaders serve the living Christ in love, aggressive faith, and prayerful humility, the people who dwell in that atmosphere become rich in the presence of God. Conversely, when a leader blatantly sins or is led into deception, the heartache of his downfall is absorbed into the spirits of those in his care.

This precept, that a leader's sin carries negative consequences, is not something with which we are unfamiliar. Do you remember what you felt when you heard of the sins of Bill Clinton, our former president? Or when Jimmy Swaggart fell? Or, consider the distress that crushes a family when a parent falls into serious iniquity. Unless it is remedied, the impact of these events is similar to that of a curse upon one's life.

Another example is seen when David ordered Joab, a general, to take a census of Israel. Joab begged the king, "Why does my lord want to do this? Why should he bring guilt on

Israel?" (1 Chron 21:3 NIV) David's sin brought "guilt on Israel" and a plague struck them, killing thousands.

Or consider the dread proclamation of Jeremiah, that "the adversary and the enemy could enter the gates of Jerusalem. Because of the sins of her prophets and the iniquities of her priests" (Lam 4:12–13). The godly example and care of true spiritual leaders, while imperfect, still creates a living shelter for the people they serve. However, when leaders vacate their post through serious sin, spiritual enemies gain access to the church that they would not otherwise have. Instead of blessedness, oppression fills the spiritual realm of that church.

So, while we may be tempted to simply ignore what happened or pretend it has not affected us, the Lord reveals in the Scriptures that He wants us to face the effects of the leader's sin and deal with its subsequent effect upon His people.

IF THE "ANOINTED PRIEST" SINS

In the Old Testament, we see this principle in the book of Leviticus. There, the Lord says, "If the anointed priest sins so as to bring guilt on the people, then let him offer to the LORD a bull without defect as a sin offering" (Lev 4:3).

"Guilt," in this context, is not a direct result of the peoples' sin. It is, however, the collective effect of what the leader's sin created within them: fear, shame, heartache, confusion and anger. The "guilt on the people" does not mean that they have sinned, but that the effect of their leader's sin has oppressed the congregation, positioning them in an "unblessable state of being."

This "unblessed state," be it anger, cynicism or confusion, as understandable as these responses may seem, is now a "guilt on the people." To return to the state of blessedness, the people now must journey away from their reaction, which needs to be openly acknowledged and atoned for.

Face the Need and Let Christ Heal

As much as they may wish it were otherwise, a wounded church often carries a discernible cloud of heaviness. For years, the influence of their wounding surfaces in mistrust of all leaders; attitudes of cynicism or fearful anticipations become part of the normal congregational thought life. Worse, their shared, unremedied pain becomes a beehive of demonic exploitation, where human attitudes of anger and confusion leave the church vulnerable to manipulation by the enemy.

The Amplified Bible, speaking of the effects, or the dwelling place, of unresolved sin, gives us an insight into this demonic infestation. It reads, "the shades of the dead are there [specters haunting the scene of past transgressions]" (Prov 9:18).

That understanding, that "specters haunt ... the scene of past transgressions," tells us that when we pass through the disappointment and heartache caused by a leader's sin, if we do not find a way to react as Christ, demons will "haunt" this scene of past transgression. Thus, our human reactions and the unresolved memories from our past can become a magnet for ongoing warfare. To move into a blessed future, we must be cleansed of the unredeemed past.

What is especially unfortunate is that the unredeemed past can be transferred to individuals who join a wounded church, even though new members were not partakers of the original wounding. New believers come to churches where mistrust of leadership has residence. Soon, through the osmosis of human relationships, the same fears, mistrust and suspicions that were resident in the older members begin to surface in the life of the new Christian.

Simply replacing pastors will not bring healing; what needs replacing is the cloud of heaviness that remains in that church. For, not only did the fallen leader need forgiveness, cleansing and renewal in Christ but, as we stated, what was transferred to the people must be cleansed as well.

Perhaps we are tempted to think, "So what? Leaders come and go. I walk with God. Their fall doesn't affect me." Individually, you may indeed be blessed; but you will never know the descent of the Lord's corporate blessing upon a healed, renewed church until you experience cleansing for the consequences of your pastor's sin.

If we fail to deal with the oppression caused by a leader's fall, it is possible that our future relationships with church leaders will be colored with fear and suspicion. The very attitude that "leaders come and go" and that one feels he or she is capable of walking alone, is itself a form of oppression. We do not have to walk alone. The voice speaking "leaders come and go" is a wounded voice. Remember: There is greater power in unity than in isolation. One may chase a thousand, but two, ten thousand. Although we may have to walk alone at times, God designed us to be interconnected members of a Christ-filled people.

Additionally, the Lord promised He will raise up "shepherds over [His people] and they will tend them; and they will not be afraid any longer, nor be terrified, nor will any be missing" (Jer 23:4). Unless we are cleansed of the effect of our negative experience, the filter of our mistrust and our corresponding isolation might disqualify us from recognizing godly leaders when the Lord brings them to us.

You see, there is a corporate blessing coming to the church which is greater than the individual blessing. The corporate blessing is greater, for it carries a unique reward to those who overcome offenses and persevere in faith for each other and their leaders. This is the Pentecost anointing that was available to the 120 in the upper room, 108 of which had to overcome the failings of the original twelve. Out of the anointing on unity, God touches multitudes, turns cities, and empowers His people with the life of heaven.

You may say, "Ours is a new church; our leaders have not fallen in sin." Locally, your church may be clean. However, the people in your church did not float from heaven to earth. They were somewhere when national leaders fell. Indeed, one does not have to be a church historian to recall how many major spiritual leaders have fallen in recent years. Each time a minister fell, the "mistrust level" toward all church leaders increased. The cumulative effect of moral failure, both on a national and local level, has smothered the fire in many Christian hearts. Some of those hearts may be sitting in your church.

If you are a pastor and you are wondering why people do not respond to your teaching as you would hope, it might be they are carrying woundedness from a previous leader. This former leader may be totally unaffiliated with your church, yet their reaction toward him is keeping them guarded and unable to truly hear from you. Among regular church attenders, this woundedness has been translated into a polite, yet numbing, attitude of unbelief and suspicion toward church leaders in general.

Remember, as a pastor or teacher, your goal is not to prepare a sermon, but to prepare a people. Thus, it is imperative that you dispel this cloud of mistrust so that people can, once again, absorb your message and be changed. Do you see this? They may not hear your teaching at the proper response level because they have distanced themselves from the memory of pain. Distance always hinders hearing.

THE CLEANSING RIVER OF FORGIVENESS

The antidote for a leader's sin in the Old Testament was to "offer to the Lord a bull without defect as a sin offering." Of course, we have a Sacrifice for sins greater than the blood of bulls and goats. Yet, until we apply Christ's sacrifice to this need, the need remains and continues to negatively affect us. Let us, therefore, present ourselves before God for examination. As we yield to His Holy Spirit, one of the great graces He pours upon us is to make all things new.

On a personal level, this renewal work is as effective as our ability to forgive those who have hurt us and let go of the heartache caused by the shortcomings of our leaders. It is a profound opportunity: we can be delivered from becoming hardened in heart. We can look forward to the future, trusting God for ever more wonderful beginnings.

Just as Daniel represented Israel in repentance before God (Dan 10), let me personally repent to you on behalf of those church leaders who have fallen or misrepresented Jesus to you. I ask for your forgiveness. Leaders have fallen and caused you distress and heartache; we have burdened you with a yoke that was not the yoke of Christ, but a yoke of oppression. For the sins of all, I ask for your forgiveness.

As God gives you grace, please release that specific man or woman who misused their spiritual authority or betrayed the solemn responsibilities entrusted to them. Again, I ask you to forgive leaders who have fallen or failed your expectations.

POSITIONED IN PRAYER

Knowing that shepherds experience a greater "striking" from the enemy (see Zech 13:7), let us also take up our positions to intercede for our leaders. God never intended that congregations would not participate in their leaders' protection, inspiration and well-being. The power and confidence in your church leadership reflects, at least in part, the answer to your prayers. Paul asked for prayer; Jesus asked for prayer, and your pastor needs your prayer as well. Unprayed-for pastors are vulnerable to the battle in unique ways. If you haven't stood in intercession for your church leaders, perhaps you are, at least in a small part, a contributor to their stumbling.

Remember, even good leaders fail. Yet, God can raise them back up again. In fact, my experience is that, in some ways, a fallen but restored leader has a depth of compassion, a "grace understanding," that makes a wonderful shepherd out of him. We should not abandon those who have fallen, but observe if their brokenness has truly attracted a new grace from God.

Remember also Daniel's words, speaking of our very days. He wrote, "And some of those who have insight will fall, in order to refine, purge, and make them pure, until the end time; because it is still to come at the appointed time" (Dan 11:35).

Through Daniel, the Holy Spirit tells us that, though certain leaders "will fall," God will not abandon them. He will, instead, "refine, purge and make them pure." Fallen leaders are difficult to bear; however, if we are part of the process of sorrow, let us also, together with Christ, be part of the restoration as well. Let us forgive our leaders for where they have failed us and, in so doing, release ourselves from the oppression of the past.

Lord, again, I forgive those leaders whose failings have caused my heart to harden. Lord, grant them, and me, new grace. Grant that we all could know Your awesome power of renewal. Father, I commit to Your hands the cleansing of my soul from the effects of fallen leaders. Restore us all into the power of Your glorious presence. In Jesus' name. Amen.

CHAPTER EIGHT

A Thankful Heart

"And let the peace of Christ rule in your hearts, to which indeed you were called in one body; and be thankful" (Col 3:15).

We can journey through life angry and proud, which manifests in slander and division, or we can become a Christian who truly represents the life of Christ. It was specifically in this regard that Paul wrote, "Rejoice always; pray without ceasing; in everything give thanks; for this is God's will for you" (1 Thess 5:16–18).

Joy, prayer and gratitude, not anger, gossip and slander, are "God's will for you." Paul is saying when you see something wrong in life, don't lose your joy over it. God is with you; His power is in you. You are heaven bound, so let the world know your faith by your joy. What you can't remedy immediately, turn over to God in prayer. Don't descend into anger. Rejoice always! Pray without ceasing! This is the positive, healing approach God gives us to life.

He continues, "In everything give thanks." We must enter the gates of God's presence with thanksgiving. Several years ago someone whom I loved very much went through a confusing time. I prayed and prayed, but soon became quietly angry at, what seemed to me, this person's slow progress. After several months, I remember praying, "Lord, I don't know why this person hasn't changed yet, but do something!" Suddenly, the presence of the Lord descended into my spirit and my eyes were opened. I saw literally dozens of answers to prayer in this individual's life! God was working, but because of my anger, I couldn't perceive the working of God.

This is why we must remain thankful. Thanksgiving is the language of faith. The moment we spend time thanking the Lord, we begin to see more clearly what He is actually doing. Our eyes open as our hearts open. I have come to realize that the "world of the ungrateful" is a world inhabited by demons.

Listen to what God's Word says:

For even though they knew God, they did not honor Him as God, or give thanks; but they became futile in their speculations, and their foolish heart was darkened. . . . And just as they did not see fit to acknowledge God any longer, God gave them over to a depraved mind, to do those things which are not proper, being filled with all unrighteousness, wickedness, greed, evil; full of envy, murder, strife, deceit, malice; they are gossips, slanderers.   —Romans 1:21, 28–30

They knew God, but did not "honor Him as God, or give thanks." As a result, God gave them over to a depraved mind. Think of it: we either have a mind that honors and thanks God or we wind up with a depraved mind, full of envy, strife, gossip and slander. The world of the ungrateful spirals ever downward until they became "futile in their speculations, and their . . .

heart was darkened." Theirs is a world in darkness. Let me say it again: if we are not attaining a thankful spirit we are slipping toward a depraved mind.

This spirit of ingratitude, of discontent and grumbling, has penetrated many throughout the body of Christ. Gossip is so prevalent in the church today it has been elevated to the status of a church tradition.

It is my passionate, focused desire to see every one of us genuinely delivered from the deception of discontent. My prayer is that each of us will rediscover the good life that God has waiting for us. If we have come to Christ, we have received every blessing in the heavenly places (Eph 1:3). But the capacity to actually *receive* God's blessings is only as functional as our ability to be truly grateful for them. Gratitude is the gateway through which God's blessings enter our lives.

So, if you are one who has a propensity toward gossip, repent. Renounce speaking evil of others. Do you want to love life and see good days? Keep your tongue from speaking evil and your lips from uttering deceit (see Ps 34:12–13). Become an intercessor. If you're in need of forgiveness for gossip, for backbiting, for slander, or for ungratefulness, this is the time.

Lord Jesus, forgive me for murmuring and complaining. When I consider that You died for my sins, that You have given me all things pertaining to life and godliness, that You have even given me Your precious Holy Spirit to guide and empower my life, I am ashamed of my carnal attitude. Forgive Me, Lord. Let the song of praise and thanksgiving toward You forever be in my mouth. Amen.

CHAPTER NINE

DECLARE WAR ON GRUMBLING

God destroyed Israel for its grumbling, murmuring and complaining against Moses. Rarely is there a church split or division that does not have, as one of its roots, a grumbling element in the church.

In a previous chapter we mentioned that, when Jesus referred to Judas Iscariot as a "devil," He was referring to the generic, impersonal definition of the word, *diabolos,* which meant "slanderer" or "malicious gossip." Judas evidently could not keep his negative perspective to himself.

Indeed, it isn't hard to imagine that, before Judas betrayed Christ, he expressed many criticisms of Jesus to the Pharisees—the final offense being that Jesus allowed a very expensive ointment to be "wasted" by being poured upon His head (see Matt 26:7). "Why was this perfume not sold for three hundred denarii, and given to poor people?" Judas asked indignantly (John 12:5).

His attitude actually led a minor insurrection toward Jesus, causing indignation to spread among the other apostles as well (see Matt 26:8). Who permitted this thoughtless luxury? Jesus did. Who reaped its immediate benefits? Again, the answer is Jesus. Perhaps, in Judas' critical mind, the last straw before betraying Jesus was that He did not apologize for this apparent "misuse of funds," but instead defended her extravagant act.

Betrayal is never a sudden thing; rather, it is an accumulative response to the unresolved anger, disappointment or jealousy one feels toward another. The offenses we do not transfer to God in surrendered prayer inevitably decay and become a poison within our spirits. This poison is then transferred to others through slander. We feel justified, yet we have actually become malicious gossips. We feel we are only serving the cause of "truth," when, in fact, we've become enemies to the cause of love.

A PROBLEM WITH GRUMBLING

To understand the betrayal of Christ, however, we must descend into its source: a grumbling spirit. When we lose sight of the many things for which we should be thankful, we become murmurers and grumblers, increasingly absorbed with a thought-life born in hell. Remember, Lucifer found fault with God in heaven! Paradise is not even enough for a grumbling spirit!

Beware when your anger toward another Christian has led you to gossip about him, especially if he's a church leader. Yes, beware: for you are no longer being conformed to Christ, but to the one who delivered Him up.

Of course, this grumbling attitude was not isolated to Judas. Many would-be disciples and Jewish leaders were also infected with it. Consider: there were miracles everywhere, and Christ has just fed the 5,000, yet a large crowd began to find fault.

"Do not grumble among yourselves," Jesus warned (John 6:43). Yet, they persisted. Remember, these were not just people who did not know Christ, but His very disciples, and they were not grumbling at a sinner, but the only sinless man who ever lived. Again, we read, "But Jesus, conscious that His disciples grumbled at this, asked, 'Does this cause you to stumble?' " (John 6:61). Yet, still the grumbling spirit continued, until "many of His disciples withdrew, and were not walking with Him anymore" (John 6:66).

Grumbling caused people to stop seeing miracles, become offended by Christ's words, and stop walking with Him. As it was then, so it is today. Grumbling will ultimately cause you to stop walking with Jesus. It is a killer. Incredibly, the early disciples (not just the Pharisees) found fault with the Son of God! They had heaven in their midst and couldn't see it. That's what a grumbling attitude can do.

This poison is prevalent in the church today. I tell you plainly: God doesn't want a grumbling people to represent Him on earth. If we are habitually gossiping, grumbling or complaining, we should beware: the path we are on leads away from Christ.

THE THANKFUL HEART

Personally, I've declared war on grumbling. I've declared an unthankful heart is an enemy to God's will. Can you join me with this? Can you crucify a murmuring spirit? We have received too much from God to allow ourselves opportunities for unbelief. We have received too many gifts and privileges to allow a grumbling, murmuring heart to disqualify us from our destiny.

In contrast, the thankful heart sees the best part of every situation. It sees problems and weaknesses as opportunities, struggles as refining tools, and sinners as saints in progress. My prayer, dear ones, is for each of us to possess the abundant life that Jesus came to give us. I want to wrestle that little, ugly grumbling thing off your soul and put a living awareness of the goodness of God in its place!

The very quality of our lives decays as we murmur. Paul warned, "Nor let us . . . grumble, as [Israel] did, and were destroyed by the destroyer" (1 Cor 10:9, 10). Every time we open ourselves to grumbling, our lives open up to destruction.

Again, Paul wrote, "Whatever is true, whatever is honorable . . . right, whatever is pure . . . lovely . . . if there is any excellence and if anything worthy of praise, let your mind dwell on these things" (Phil 4:8).

If your mind is fixed on something other than the wonderful life of God, it's not "fixed," it's broken. God wants to give us a new attitude. You say, "Who's going to take care of finding all the things that are wrong?" Oh, there are plenty of volunteers for that. Better to ask, "How can I attain the blessed life Jesus came to give me?"

A BLESSED FAMILY AND FUTURE

We must learn to be thankful for the people God has given us. Some of you cannot communicate with your loved ones. Why? Part of the reason is that we are unappreciative of them. You see, just as God requires we "enter His gates with thanksgiving" (Ps 100:4), so we gain access and the "right to speak" into the hearts of our loved ones through genuinely appreciating the good things we see within them.

For example, if you're not thankful for your teenagers, your disappointment with them will ultimately drive them from you. Take time with them and sincerely communicate the things you appreciate about them. There are many good things about them that they need to hear you acknowledge. I am not saying we shouldn't correct our children, but that we must balance correction with appreciation and praise, reinforcing their sense of self worth and value.

Because God has created us to be social creatures, we are born with an inner desire for acceptance. In fact, we desire acceptance more than we seek for righteousness. By appreciating our loved ones, we affirm and settle the search for acceptance that compels them toward ungodly associations. Just as when property "appreciates," increasing in value, so when we appreciate our loved ones, destructive tendencies created by self-hatred and fear of rejection are removed. We inspire them to become better, not by continually harping on what's wrong with them, but by clearly appreciating and establishing what is right.

There's something like radar inside the human heart that senses the displeasure of others. Displeasure and ingratitude are like a repellant to human relationships. People think, "If I can't measure up, if you can't see anything good in me, I'll go where people will accept me as I am." Thanksgiving brings our loved ones closer to us rather than driving them away.

Speaking of the people the Father put in His life, Jesus prayed, "Thine they were, and thou gavest them me" (John 17:6 KJV). One translation reads, "They are your gift to me" (NAB). Jesus didn't think of His disciples as always falling short, or as a hindrance; rather, He welcomed them into His life as a gift of His Father's love. Did they fail Him? Yes. But He was thankful and treated them with reverence and gratitude.

Your loved ones, your pastor and church are gifts from God. Tell them you appreciate them. Personally, I am deeply thankful to God for my wife and her love and support. Likewise, I thank God for my children and the people I serve at my church; our pastors, elders and deacons are wonderful people. Are any of them perfect? No, but I appreciate them as gifts from the hand of God Himself.

However, I know married couples who, every time they talk intimately, continually wind up discussing what's wrong with their relationship. Why not stop talking about it and just do what's right? Do you understand? Ingratitude is "relationship repellant." Thanksgiving, on the other hand, is the doorway to oneness.

Truly, we ought to be the happiest, most joyful, earthshaking individuals the world has ever seen. God is for us. He's written our names in the Book of Life. That alone is more than enough to make us invincibly thankful, happy, glad and joyful.

Some of you have been gossiping and grumbling. It's time for a fast. From what? From grumbling. For the next thirty days, each time you're tempted to complain, find something for which to be thankful. Make lists of people and things that you are thankful to God for. Let's put an end to grumbling and complaining and become a people who possess the wonderful life of God!

Lord, deliver me from words that carry gossip. Master, I realize that I, too, at times have betrayed You when I gossiped and grumbled about other Christians. Jesus, create in me a passion to walk in thanksgiving and praise to You. Free me to be an encourager to others. Amen.

CHAPTER TEN

PASTORAL
SAFEGUARDS
AGAINST DIVISION

Pastors, too often we are the cause of the problems in our churches. We are too insecure. We can't expect a congregation to trust us if we do not trust the Lord. It is time for us to grow up and, by God's grace, make room for the church to grow as well.

To the senior pastor or leader: How do we remedy the relational tragedy of divisions and church splits? Certainly, the complexities involved in solving this sin require more information than can be found in a single book. There are, indeed, many issues and numerous angles to consider. What I have compiled here are some fundamental standards that will help preserve your church from unnecessary divisions.

1. Make it easier for people to transfer to another church. As pastors, admittedly, it is difficult to let people go. However, because we do not provide creative, gracious ways for people to move on, left with no alternative, they feel forced to rebel against us. In war, even enemies exchange prisoners; how much more should the body of Christ implement loving ways to release individuals? Remember, God thought it fitting that there would be four gospels, four different ways of expressing the good news of Jesus Christ. Likewise, people need variety. So, beware when your insecurities make it hard for people to move on.

2. Provide a clear understanding of the spiritual authority structure in your church. Some of us feel awkward teaching about our authority as pastors. Yet, we will have problems if we are vague about our church government. You don't have to be "authoritarian" to teach on authority. God gives us authority to protect, guide, correct and console those whom we love. We have authority to liberate, but not dominate. So, let the church understand why Christ gives leaders authority and why it is important to their growth to submit to those leaders and obey them (see Heb 13:17).

   The flow of authority should be plainly stated in a brochure or handout that people receive when they join the church. During times of turbulence, clarity concerning the governmental structure can help people to avoid siding with those engendering division.

3. Before accepting a call to a local church, make sure you understand where final authority resides in that church. In some churches, directional leadership does not rest with the pastor, but with the elder or deacon board. On occasion, this board is not seeking a senior leader as much as someone who is a good teacher, counselor or administrator. Then, when a division arises concerning a change in church

direction, the pastor himself splits the church. This is very wrong.

No minister should accept the call to serve a local congregation without also accepting the unique flow of authority in that church. The authority structure should be spelled out clearly in the beginning so there is no misunderstanding.

4. Be honest about your intended use of spiritual gifts. I have known pastors who actually lied when asked by the call committee if they spoke in tongues. Then, after a few months of guiding the church, they introduced spiritual gifts against the will of the deacon board. This is a church split waiting to happen.

5. Be accountable to a board or leadership team. Any pastor who does not have a board of elders or deacons, or a district supervisor to whom he submits, is asking for division. At the very least, a pastor should willingly be accountable concerning his moral behavior and doctrine. Additionally, that same leadership team should watch for fatigue or stress in the pastor or the pastor's family. Pastor, just as you expect your church to submit to your vision and guidance, so should you render yourself genuinely accountable to those who can advise, strengthen and balance your spiritual walk.

6. Be willing to listen to the advice or suggestions of church members. Some of the best advice I have ever received came from housewives in the church. Sometimes, what seems like a complaint from a member may actually be the voice of the Lord trying to show us an area of need that we haven't addressed. So, model humility and openness. It will cut down on members feeling they need to form a posse just to communicate with you.

7. Deal with your insecurities. Paul tells us that God has given a variety of ministries to equip the saints. None of us can

meet every human need. Consider how doctors will send a patient to a specialist—one who is better qualified to remedy a unique physical condition than they are. They are not so insecure that they cannot enlist another doctor to better serve their patients. They recognize their limits and get help.

Likewise, we need to admit that we cannot cure or fix every spiritual condition people have in our churches. If another local pastor has an effective ministry in a certain area, do not be reluctant to send a member to that pastor.

8. Unite with other pastors in the city for prayer, fellowship and healing. God is restoring unity to the citywide church. We can hardly expect our local flock to not divide if we ourselves are divided from the larger body of Christ. We need friends and confidants, people with whom we can be vulnerable and transparent with our needs.

   Often ministers will suffer the loss of close church friends who, for one reason or another, actually turn against them. To survive, pastors will pray, "If I have to walk alone, Lord, I will follow You." Such a prayer is helpful during the time of heartache, but it can become like an inner vow which creates a wall of isolation around the minister's heart. We learn to walk alone, as it is less painful; however, it is also less fruitful. It is thus imperative that leaders unite with other pastors, where trust and healing can emerge and pastors themselves can be healed.

9. Be prepared for people in the church to desire ministry opportunities. If our teaching is truly anointed of God, people will grow. How much they will grow depends upon the size of their opportunity. Goldfish, in a little bowl, will grow two or so inches; in a pond, they might grow as large as ten or twelve inches. It's the size of the opportunity that often determines the level of growth. As leaders, we should be aware that maturing Christians need opportunities to

develop spiritually. How have we provided sanctioned ministry opportunities for upcoming leaders? Are we connected to ministry schools where individuals can receive further training? These positive approaches will help people grow without splitting the church.

10. Walk with integrity. I mentioned the following truth in an earlier chapter, but it is worthy of repeating. The Scriptures tell of a time when God's people were taken captive by the Babylonians. As Jeremiah lamented the destruction of Jerusalem, he made an insightful, yet frightening statement. He wrote, "the adversary and the enemy could enter the gates of Jerusalem. Because of the sins of her prophets and the iniquities of her priests" (Lam 4:12–13).

    Habitual, serious sin in your life leaves the church you serve vulnerable to spiritual assault. True spiritual authority is a shelter, comfort and strength to God's people. While no one is perfect, if we walk with serious compromise, the enemy will gain access to our churches "through the sins of her prophets and the iniquities of her priests." What we are fighting outwardly may be what we ourselves caused inwardly by the strongholds of sin in our lives. Perhaps this truth seems too hard to bear, but David's sins caused a plague to fall on Israel and not until he offered sacrifice in repentance did the plague abate.

11. Stay close to God. Remember, all ministry is first unto the Lord. If you have suffered a church split, your heart probably has been wounded and is in need of healing. Every one whom God has used has passed through difficulties, suffering rejection, slander and betrayal. Though our hearts are struck and wounded, yet the Lord desires to restore us and, in all these things, make us more than conquerors. Just as the Lord restored David's soul, as you draw near to Him, He will restore yours as well (see Psalm

23). Take time with Christ daily. After all, this is really about your relationship with Him.

Lord, You said the good shepherd lays down his life for the sheep. Master, I desire to be a good shepherd, one who feeds and cares for Your flock. Lord, heal my heart where I've been wounded or become cautious. Let my soul be free to love You fully and serve those You have committed to my care. In Jesus' name. Amen.

— CHAPTER ELEVEN —

A GOD OF ORDER

"For this reason I left you in Crete, that you might set in order what remains" (Titus 1:5).

I want to talk about a prominent aspect of the Father's nature and our corresponding need to understand the realm of authority. For some, the mere mention of the word authority awakens fear, so before we begin, let me ask you for grace. If possible, please consider what I present without forming your opinion until I'm done.

THE VALUE OF FREEDOM

Before we discuss authority, I want to counterbalance my words with another truth concerning our spiritual freedom in Christ. First, when the Spirit of God begins His transforming work, He starts with individuals. We are not faceless numbers to the Father, but beloved children. Indeed, Jesus assures us that His sheep know His voice as He calls them each by name.

As unique souls, we are important to the Lord. He hears our individual cries when we pray; He knows our unique needs when we struggle. As individuals, we are valued by God. The Father's original purpose was to make us in His image; at the core of the divine nature is true, spiritual freedom. As Paul wrote, "It was for freedom that Christ set us free" (Gal 5:1).

We will misunderstand what this chapter is about unless we read it as spiritually free people. God does not want us to "look" outwardly righteous, yet inwardly be in bondage. He wants us free, in bondage to no one or any thing but God Himself. You see, if our righteousness is only because the pastor or other Christians are looking, we are shallow indeed. Jesus came to set captives free and bring liberty to prisoners. God wants us to be individuals who, in the power of the Holy Spirit, have control over our mind, will and emotions. He especially does not want us subservient to the intimidations or manipulations of man.

The Father sets us perfectly free so, in true freedom, we can choose conformity to the Son of God. Christlikeness is our choice, our liberty, and our destiny.

Therefore, when we discuss order, authority and submission issues, I pray that you hear my words as free people who have a clear vision of becoming Christlike. As such, you have the right to go to any church or no church at all; you are free to throw this book against a wall or read only what you want. No one can exclude you from their church because, from the moment you were born again, God enrolled you in the "church of the first-born," which is in heaven (see Heb 12:22–23).

But, it is one thing to be assured of salvation; it is another to attain the likeness of Christ. If we will, in truth, become Christlike, we must see with revelation the reasons why our Father calls us to honor the order in our local church and why the way to exercising Christlike authority is bowing in Christlike submission.

GOD HONORS ORDER AND AUTHORITY

Having secured ourselves in the freedom given us in Christ, let us turn our eyes upon the Father. One cannot truly know God nor appreciate Him as He is without being awed at the ordered array of His universe. The life we enjoy in its splendor and variety is built upon a substructure of immutable order. The God who created animals, vegetation and people also created the subatomic worlds and the unchanging laws of physics.

When something is "ordered," it's because someone is in authority. We may imagine ourselves in the afterlife enjoying the great pleasures of heaven, but there is authority in heaven. Heaven itself is ordered with an angelic hierarchy that includes archangels, seraphim, cherubim, thrones, dominions, principalities, powers, virtues and angels. Each of these spirit-beings represents a level of authority in God's kingdom. Remember, heaven is not like earth. Most of earth's population follows their own will as they decide life's choices; in heaven, only one will is done: God's. If you don't like this idea, you can't go to heaven, for only those who do God's will are going to enter the kingdom of God (see Matt 7:21).

Of course, doing God's will unites the reason we were created with the joy of serving the Creator. God matches our gifts and skills with opportunities to fulfill them; and while we accomplish the tasks we were created to fulfill, we cannot help but worship Him. But still, only one will is done.

I am saying this because this same God of order, who created the ordered universe and the hierarchy of angels in heaven, also conceived and designed the church. In fact, originally "church" was an extension of God's ordered domain: the kingdom of heaven on earth. Thus, when we read the book of Acts, we see that the people in the early church were part of this ordered domain: united "with one mind" and "with one accord"(Acts 1:14; Acts 4:24, 32; 5:12). Because heaven is ordered, and the Lord is a God of order, the church was an ordered society where authority and submission were simply accepted on earth as it is in heaven.

One may argue, "If we had their power, we'd be united as well." Let me emphasize, they were of one mind *before* Pentecost (see Acts 1:14). If there had not been unity among the disciples prior to Pentecost, there would not have been an outpouring of the Holy Spirit on Pentecost. The outpouring did not create unity; unity made the way for the outpouring. The order was first, then came the power of the Spirit.

This principle of having order before power can also be seen by studying the Israelites who conquered Canaan, and also David, who with his mighty men united Israel and extended her boundaries. In both cases, unity preceded power. Central to the empowering of people to attain their destiny was their ability to submit to the leaders God had appointed. There simply cannot be sustainable unity without authority and submission.

Let me take this a little further. While the Lord sits in the heavens and does whatever He pleases, yet repeatedly the Scriptures confirm that it pleases the Lord to honor the order He creates and work within its protocols. Consider: the Lord appeared to Paul, spoke to him, actually blinded him in His glory, and then said, "Rise, and enter the city, and it shall be told you what you must do" (Acts 9:6).

Why didn't the Lord just tell Paul what he had to do? Paul would have to learn about God, at least initially, as he submitted to other Christian leaders. This is God's order and the Lord Himself honored it. Paul had to hear about Jesus from Ananias, a man who was a Christian before him.

Or consider Cornelius: an angel appeared to this Roman centurion in a dream and told him that a man named Simon Peter would explain to him the way of salvation. Why didn't the angel simply tell Cornelius about Jesus? Cornelius would be the first European convert, but God had begun the church with the Jews. Before the Gentiles could enter the kingdom en masse they would hear of Christ from the Jews, who first accepted the Messiah. God honored the order He created, which was to present the gospel "to the Jew first and also to the Greek" (Rom 1:16; 2:10).

Consider church protocol in the book of Acts. When Philip brought the gospel to Samaria, miracles, conversions and great signs were accomplished. But Philip would not lay his hands upon the Samaritans to receive the Holy Spirit. Why? Because until this time, the Holy Spirit had only spread through the hands of the first apostles. Again, God required His servant to respect the order and authority of the first apostles.

Or consider the order in Jesus' family. The angel Gabriel spoke to Mary, revealing that, through the Holy Spirit, she would conceive the Son of God. Yet, from the time Mary married Joseph, God spoke only to him concerning direction for the family. Angels assured him Mary's pregnancy was from God; he received dreams and angelic warnings, telling him to leave Israel and warnings that instructed him when to return.

God honored the order of the family—because Adam was created first, then Eve. Yes, the Lord still works when conditions are out of order, because He honors faith. But just because He accommodates our weaknesses, we should not assume He will endorse them with the fulness of His power.

Consider the life of Christ Himself. As a child, He grew up "in subjection" to His parents (see Luke 2:51). He also was submissive to the instructions of the rabbis and, as was His custom, He faithfully participated in the Sabbath readings at the synagogue (see Luke 4:16). Jesus simply was not a rebel. At the Jordan River, He submitted Himself to the ministry of John the Baptist, though He was John's spiritual superior. Yet, to "fulfill all righteousness," He eagerly submitted Himself. *Indeed, it was while He humbled Himself to a lesser ministry that the flood of the Father's pleasure, together with the Holy Spirit, descended upon Him* (see Matt 3:13–17).

I know what I am about to say will seem over the line to many, but Jesus did not instruct His followers to rebel even against false religious authority. Listen to what He taught, "The scribes and the Pharisees have seated themselves in the chair of Moses." On their own, the Pharisees assumed an authority that God had not given them. Yet listen to how Jesus tells His disciples to relate to false authority: "therefore all that they tell you, do and observe, but do not do according to their deeds; for they say things, and do not do them" (Matt 23:2–3).

Amazingly, Jesus instructed both His disciples and the larger multitude to "do and observe" all that the Pharisees taught. I don't believe in any way He intended for His disciples to remain with the Pharisees, but the implication in Jesus' statement is this: as long as you are Jewish and attending temple services, the Pharisees are in charge and here's how to relate. Submit to them, but do not become like them.

Even though their authority was questionable and their behavior hypocritical, He did not say to disrespect them, but rather to not do as they do. Yes, Jesus Himself confronted the Pharisees harshly. However, Jesus was not raising up a people to be known for their confrontational attitudes; they were to be known for their strength of character and their love.

Again, when Jesus stood before Pilate, He showed Himself meek, like a lamb. Pilate challenged Him, " 'Do You not know that I have authority to release You, and I have authority to crucify You?' Jesus answered, 'You would have no authority over Me, unless it had been given you from above' " (John 19:10–11).

Jesus knew that all authority in the universe—the very realm of authority—was under the domain of the Father's watchful gaze (see Rom 13:1). While authority itself could be misused, still the Father's authority transcended human authority and could, with great power, override the imperfections of man. Thus, Jesus was not afraid to submit to people who were spiritually less than Himself because He knew God's greater authority would transform injustice to justice.

In the Godhead, the Father exists as God in authority; the Son exists as God in submission. Jesus, you recall, only did the things He saw the Father do; everything about Christ was an act of obedience and submission. Christ reveals how God submits to God. In this submission is peace; Jesus rested in the Father's watchful gaze. The issues were never between Jesus and other men, but between Himself and the Father.

When Jesus suffered the injustice of His trial, He didn't blame Pilate, the Pharisees, His disciples or the multitudes. He didn't even blame the devil. Instead, Peter tells us that while Jesus was "being reviled, He did not revile in return; while suffering, He uttered no threats, but kept entrusting Himself to Him who judges righteously" (1 Peter 2:23).

Peter uses Christ's example of submission to tell the church, "Keep your behavior excellent among the Gentiles . . . Submit yourselves for the Lord's sake to every human institution, whether to a king as the one in authority, or to governors as sent by him for the punishment of evildoers and the praise of those who do right" (1 Peter 2:12–14).

He continues, "Act as free men, and do not use your freedom as a covering for evil, but use it as bondslaves of God. Honor all men; love the brotherhood, fear God, honor the king. Servants, be submissive to your masters with all respect, not only to those who are good and gentle, but also to those who are unreasonable" (1 Peter 2:16–18).

Did Christ's faith work? Of course! In the first century the cross was the symbol of torture, death and utter hopelessness. Because Jesus trusted the Father's authority to override the misuse of authority, the cross today is the symbol of redemption, resurrection and hope.

Beloved, the Lord is a God of order and, for His purposes, He requires we submit to authority and order, whether it's in the secular world, the family or the church. Listen carefully: rebellion is not a virtue. Submission was clearly the pattern in Jesus' life. He revealed how God would submit to God and, in so doing, set the pattern for us, who are created in His image.

Lord, forgive me for my insolence toward those in authority. I confess that I have not trusted nor understood the realm of authority, but I ask that You forgive me. Help me to ever keep my eyes upon You, trusting Your ability to take my submitted, believing heart through every injustice and into the realm of redemption and power. In Jesus' name. Amen.

CHAPTER TWELVE

CHRISTLIKE
SUBMISSION

Our submission to authority is not born of fear nor intimidation. True submission comes from revelation and an understanding of the character of Jesus Christ. It is a means of rapid growth and imparted grace.

J esus had full possession of His soul; He didn't react to man; He fully trusted God. Thus, He could submit to man's frail systems and miscarriages of authority, knowing the Father would ultimately judge righteously and transform the injustice. Where Lucifer demanded full independence from the authority of God, Jesus was perfectly yielded to the Father's authority (2 Cor 13:4).

Now, I know that some are afraid to embrace a submissive attitude of heart. They worry that they'll have to blindly submit to the antichrist or be forced, cult-like, into all manner of sin, including sexual. We have only to consider the recent sex scandals in the Catholic Church and the misuse of authority among the priests to shudder with legitimate concern.

So, let me reinforce this truth: Jesus never submitted to authority that would cause Him to sin, nor did He expect His disciples to sin if one in authority ordered them. Just as you *choose* to submit, so you *choose* to not submit to one telling you to sin. If your employer asks you to lie for him, you can maintain a submissive attitude while telling him, "No, I can't do that." Yet, even here our motive is not to rebel against man, but to submit on a higher level to God.

Another fear is that, by submitting to another person, we will lose ourselves and become like them. In fact, when we submit to the anointing upon a person, we gain more than we invest. Elisha received a double portion of Elijah's anointing because he passionately and faithfully submitted himself to his mentor's anointing. Bear in mind, Elijah was the opposite personality type of Elisha. Yet, by submitting, he doubled the accomplishments of Elijah.

You see, what we possess of spiritual power is already ours, but it is limited. By putting ourselves in submission to another, we gain some measure of the other person's anointing. Elisha did not lose his own identity by submitting; he did not become a "little Elijah." He still retained his own personality and approach to ministry except, when his ministry began, he had twice as much power.

We fear that by being submissive, we will be asked to give more than we receive. Again, the opposite is true. Jesus taught, "He who receives a prophet in the name of a prophet shall receive a prophet's reward" (Matt 10:41). Submission is the vehicle for receiving. God rewards a prophet, not only in the world to come, but also here. The "prophet's reward" represents the unique power dimension a man or woman of God has purchased with sacrifice and suffering. Just by submitting ourselves, by humbly "receiving" from them, we can obtain without cost a measure of the prophet's reward.

Remember: the multitudes did not know Jesus was the Son of God; they didn't understand "by His stripes" they would be healed (Isa 53:5 NKJV). They did just one thing: they submitted to Christ for healing and received the "prophet's reward." The Pharisees, on the other hand, did not receive Christ; thus, their unsubmitted attitude disqualified them from receiving the benefits of Jesus' power.

When a church submits to me, I assume an added responsibility. It does not mean that I, as a leader, control their now mindless lives. How opposite the truth is! A person submitted to my authority is one for whom I pray more frequently; when they are sick, I visit them. When they weep, I cry with them; and where they are immature, I give myself to training them, instructing them in the mysteries of life. The submitted person is the beneficiary of the relationship, much more than the one in authority.

We have seen the abuses of authority, and it has made many of us wary and resistant to the true benefits of submission and impartation. But let's take this a step further. You do not need to actually have a man or woman of God in front of you to be submitted to their anointing. When I was a young man and new in Christ, I would take books by Andrew Murray or Watchman Nee, then kneel at the foot of my bed and read their words. I often felt that I was drinking in, through the Holy Spirit, the substance of their anointing. You see, I didn't just read their words, I submitted myself to their teaching.

So, consider submission to be the free choice of a wise person who sees something Christlike in another's life and has asked to receive it. Submission does not diminish us; it doubles us. It extends the boundaries of our spirituality into the lives of people whom we see were transformed by Christ—and allows what they have received from Him to be imparted to us as well.

Lord, what a storehouse of riches Your church is! To think that when You ascended on high, You gave gifts to men, spiritual leaders, who could advance my spiritual growth simply by my submission. Master, let my eyes be ever on You and let me follow men only as they follow You. Amen.

CHAPTER THIRTEEN

THE POWER OF BIBLICAL HONOR

Practice showing honor for just one month to those in authority over you and to those in submission to you: Honor will transform your world.

I n a world where "every intent of the thoughts of [mankind's] heart was only evil continually" (Gen 6:5), Noah walked "blameless in his time" (Gen 6:9). Noah was a righteous man whose integrity and depth of character was a contradiction to his culture.

Noah faithfully resisted temptation and the pressure to sin; he preached righteousness and spoke boldly against evil. Aware that the end of his world was near, most commentators say he continued preaching repentance for one hundred and twenty years. Throughout his life, he never wavered; although his words converted no one, he never quit. Among all who lived in his generation, Noah alone found favor with God.

Consider also: Noah's eyes beheld the terrible descent of the wrath of God; his ears heard the terrifying, final cries of an entire civilization. His mind experienced the horrifying destruction of every man, woman and child outside the ark. What burden does such an experience create upon the human soul? What nightmares?

We don't know how Noah processed the catastrophic end of his world, but here's what we do know: After the flood, a second genesis began with Noah. He farmed and planted a vineyard. From the harvest he produced juice, which fermented into wine. We don't know if this was the first time he, or any man, tasted the effects of wine, but we do know that he drank it and it made him so drunk that he collapsed in his tent, unconscious and naked in a drunken stupor (see Gen 9:20–21).

Here was a righteous preacher who, for whatever reason, had fallen short of his own high standards. Into this scene comes Ham, one of his three sons. Ham entered Noah's tent and saw the shameful state his father was in. Instead of silently covering his father, Ham reported the scene to his two brothers. Ham's motive was not to discreetly cover his father's shame, but rather to expose it (v 22).

His brothers, Shem and Japheth, the Scriptures tell us, were of a different spirit. They took a garment and, walking backward with it on their shoulders, they covered their father. Keep this point in mind: Ham dishonored his father by seeking to expose his shame; Shem and Japheth honored their father by covering his weakness. When Noah discovered what occurred, he cursed Ham's descendants because of what Ham had done; blessings and prosperity, he proclaimed, would light upon Shem and Japheth (vv 23–27).

The lesson for us is profound: Our future and the future of our children is attached to how well we understand the value of honor and the curse that follows us when we exploit the imperfections of those in authority over us.

AMERICAN CULTURE

I want to talk to you about honor and dishonor in America. Let me state beforehand, though, that I love America, I fast for this nation, and I carry an unceasing burden of prayer for her and her leaders. When some Christians have, in the past, anticipated America's destruction, I have wept for America's revival. I believe Americans are a generous, often self-sacrificing, freedom-loving people. Additionally, this nation has stood with Israel and has extended its hands to the poor of the world. I also believe many of our forefathers were Christians who, as they knelt upon the sands of the New World, dedicated this land and its future to God.

Yet, frankly, America's love for freedom has led us across moral boundaries. Today, we demand, and our courts protect, all manner of immorality under free speech provisions. The unborn are denied the freedom of life itself for the sake of a woman's "freedom of choice." Our insatiable lusts have created a caricature of freedom that is unbalanced by responsibility and untempered by heaven's authority. For many, we are not "One Nation Under God," but "One Nation Under Freedom." Increasingly, in America, freedom has become its own god.

Some of this can be tracked to the justifiable reaction of our founding fathers as they rebelled against the tyranny of European kings and bishops. Reaching to create a land free of authoritarianism certainly was noble. However, in our rejection of the cultural traditions of the past, we have minimized the power of honor that existed in older cultures.

Consider: Nations are not only governed by laws, but also unique societal mores. For instance, in Asian nations, honor and respect preside over their societies; people bow when greeting as a sign of honor. For Germanic nations, discipline and obedience set boundaries. For Americans, liberty is the identifying trait. Yet, when the core standard of a people is freedom itself, whatever virtues restrain freedoms (such as self-denial, honor or compliance) often are devalued as flaws.

As a result, a society that learns to minimize honor, minimizes the positive effect the principles of honor have upon its basic institutions. It is precisely because of the lack of honor that our institutions of family, church, and school have suffered unprecedented breakdowns over the past half century.

THE GADSDEN FLAG

The early pioneers came to America looking for the New World. Their DNA remains a constant motive in the American psyche: *Americans are still looking for a new world.* We tend to live at the frontier of change: new ideas, new philosophies and trends. Today, in many ways, we have become one huge reaction to authority and tradition. We are not happy unless we are pushing the boundaries and breaking the limits. "No rules" has become the rallying cry for a spirit that infects our culture.

In truth, the seeds of this defiant attitude were sown long ago, even before this nation officially broke with England. Consider the Gadsden Flag. During the Revolutionary War, perhaps more than any other, this flag embodied the sentiment of many patriots, as they carried it into more battles than other flags. In fact, Benjamin Franklin pushed to have this flag represent the spirit of the new republic. What was the Gadsden Flag? It was a coiled serpent with the inscription, "Don't tread on me."

You will recall that Jesus specifically told His disciples they would "tread upon serpents" (Luke 10:19). Christ's statement is a reference to the Garden of Eden, where the Lord promised that the seed of the woman, Christ, would tread upon the head of the serpent. Yet, woven into the fabric of the American culture is this brazen defiance: "Don't tread on me." Was this banner merely the symbol of rebellion against England or did it embody a rebellion against anyone, including Christ Himself?

Even among the early American Christians, there existed a strong independent heart attitude. Most of our first ancestors came from "Protestant" stock; they were "those who protest." Not only had they protested the perceived errors of Catholicism but, during various eras, Protestants persecuted and protested each other as well. Their legacy of visible, vocal dissent as a means of change has been structured into America's subconsciousness so that, even today, to protest is to walk a heroic path. It is to follow those who, for the sake of their principles—and often at the cost of their lives—defied the authority of a king or bishop.

Thus, confrontation emerged in America as a means through which change materialized. Let us not fail to defend the virtue that fearlessly speaks against true evil. Yet, too often we find ourselves protesting when we could have humbly and civilly discussed issues that need change.

I am saying that "confrontational spirituality" has been carried to excess in the church and often is the spark that ignites the fire of division and splits. I am not denying that there are times we need to confront a situation or person. But there are far too many of us who, thinking we are the spiritual sons of the Old Testament prophets, are simply critical and confrontational by nature.

This is especially troublesome when we consider New Testament Scriptures which, in fact, call us to the exact opposite approach in our relationships. God calls us to honor and respect people, even when we disagree with them. Consider this admonition from Peter:

> Honor all men; love the brotherhood, fear God, honor the king. Servants, be submissive to your masters with all respect. —1 Peter 2:17–18a

Honor all men? Honor the king? Servants be submissive with respect? Surely this apostolic leader is not speaking to the church in America! We want our rights! We are not afraid of any man, be he king or priest. Yes, but the issue is not whether we are afraid; it is whether we are capable of showing genuine honor in obedience to God's Word.

There is something within us that grates at the idea of honoring people. We say, often quite righteously, we will only honor God. We feel it is our task to keep others humble, lest their pride take over. In reality, it is our pride that has taken over, not theirs; it is fueled by our jealousy of another's success.

God calls us to honor all men for the simple fact that He chose to give them life. Jesus lived and died so sinful men could be saved. People are precious to the Father. Yes, today the person standing before you may be a sinner, but by showing honor you tell that person that he or she is important to the Almighty.

Some people we honor for their attainments; others, we honor for their intrinsic worth to God. Yet, the call of God is to honor all. Not that we honor the actions of sinners, but the humanity of sinners. We are not to worship people, as those who swoon over celebrities; but we are to show all men honor.

You cannot lead someone to Christ whom you have dishonored. You cannot sincerely communicate the love of God if you do not respect the person to whom you are speaking. Our tradition of dishonoring people has not come from God. In fact, the kingdom of God emerges with a completely opposite spirit. The kingdom is a culture graced with honor and respect for the dignity of all people, which Jesus demonstrated repeatedly by the honor He showed the often maligned Samaritans.

Consider: within the body of Christ we are commanded to honor every member, actually giving to the "unseemly members" more abundant honor (1 Cor 12:23–24). As stated, we are also called to "honor all men" and "honor the king" (1 Peter 2:17). We are additionally required to honor the church elders (1 Tim 5:17); and at work, we should honor and respect those who are our employers (1 Tim 6:1). We are to honor widows

(1 Tim 5:3), spouses (1 Peter 3:7, Eph 5:33 AMP), the unseemly (1 Cor 12:23–25) and the aged (Lev 19:32). In fact, when the gray-headed enter a room we are told to stop talking, stand, and acknowledge with reverence the entrance of the older individual (Lev 19:32). When was the last time that happened in America?

The Lord Himself bestows honor on people. John 12:26 says, "If anyone serves Me, the Father will honor him." And Psalm 91:14–15 says, "Because he has loved Me . . . I will rescue him, and honor him." So if the Lord has no problem honoring people, considering His great glory, why are we so apt to dishonor each other?

The word *honor* in the Greek meant "to fix valuation, esteem by implication and to revere." Picture a home where the children revere their parents and the husband and wife honor each other. We must esteem and fix value to each other. For honor creates a spiritual buffer against the enemy's attacks, which otherwise erode the quality of our lives.

Moreover, honor releases the power of God, while dishonor greatly hinders it. Jesus taught, " 'A prophet is not without honor except in his home town, and in his own household.' And He did not do many miracles there because of their unbelief" (Matt 13:57–58). The people of Jesus' hometown did not honor Him, and their lack of honor, Jesus called "unbelief," for which cause He could do no miracles. In other words, when we dishonor a man or woman of God, we shut down the power of God from working through them.

THE ABILITY TO ADVANCE IN LIFE

Paul reminds us of the fourth commandment. He writes, "Honor your father and mother (which is the first commandment with a promise), that it may be well with you" (Eph 6:2–3). With that truth in mind, let's return to the story about Noah. When Ham exposed his father, Noah cursed Canaan, the son of Ham. Why didn't Noah curse Ham instead of Ham's son? As Ham had been to Noah, so Canaan would be to Ham. Noah's curse was profound. He said Canaan would be "a servant of servants" (Gen 9:25). Why? Because if you can't honor an imperfect leader, you will have continual difficulty advancing in life. You will always be wrestling with poverty.

You see, there are no leaders other than imperfect leaders. Your employer or boss, your pastor or teacher, your mayor, or your father or mother—they are all imperfect. When we expose them to humiliation or dishonor by telling others of their weaknesses, it brings a curse upon us. We will never advance in life with such an attitude.

To be successful, we need to be able to submit to leaders who are imperfect without dishonoring them. Again, I am not saying we are to submit to leaders who have committed serious sexual sin or crimes worthy of imprisonment, but we should not have qualms about submitting to men and women who are simply imperfect.

You say, "If I do that, I will feel like a hypocrite, a 'yes' man." If you don't show honor, you are already a hypocrite. For a true Christian esteems and respects people; you don't have to trust them, but you must honor and respect them.

Now this doesn't mean you shouldn't have concerns when you see a problem. You may indeed have good advice or even a revelation to share that can help your leader. But don't open the door to dishonoring leaders, especially in the church! If you see a problem, don't follow Ham's example. Don't go telling your brothers; instead, cover the situation in love. Follow the procedure Jesus gives us in Matthew 18, remaining respectful and humble as you seek to bring an end to sin in a person's life.

Perhaps you have difficulty advancing in life. It is possible that you had a dishonoring spirit toward your parents, teachers or others in authority over you and, in a moment of anger, they spoke a curse over you ("You are a loser, you will never amount to anything"). You have been blaming them, but the real cause has been your dishonoring attitude.

Today, that curse can be broken. Ask God to forgive you for not relating with honor to imperfect authority. Learn to pray for those over you when you see their imperfections, covering them with the blood of Christ. Become one who covers instead of exposing their weakness.

Remember, the future generations of Ham became slaves. How you relate to the imperfections of those in authority determines not only your future, but also the future of your children and your children's children. Do they hear you complain about your boss? Do they listen when you criticize your pastor? Is a curse being passed on to them when they are forced by proximity to hear you slander those in authority? Do you see this? You are actually teaching them how to *not* succeed in life. A dishonoring spirit will cause them to remain needy, frustrated and outside the realm of the blessed and prosperous.

Instead, when there is a need you see in a leader, pray for that person. Let your children see you praying, and demonstrate how they can handle the imperfects of life.

Right now, your children are patterning their lives after you. They are learning how to deal with the imperfections of life from you. Will they become bitter and angry at life's structure of authority? Or will they be free to relate to imperfect authorities over them, and do so with honor? Are you breeding generations of slaves or generations of free men and women?

Lord Jesus, we see how You honored the poor, the sick and the downtrodden. You also did not turn away Your disciples or shame them when they failed. Instead, You empowered Your leaders with Your covering love and asked them to show that same love to others. Lord, grant us the grace to honor all men, and so reveal Your love to our world. Amen.

CHAPTER FOURTEEN

ARE YOU CURRENTLY IN A CHURCH SPLIT?

"For I am afraid that perhaps when I come I may find you to be not what I wish and may be found by you to be not what you wish; that perhaps there may be strife, jealousy, angry tempers, disputes, slanders, gossip, arrogance, disturbances" (2 Cor 12:20).

If you are considering splitting your church, then I suggest you set up special seating in your new sanctuary, for you are about to make permanent residents of the spirits of strife, anger and suspicion. They may not show up immediately but, with limited exceptions, these spirits will abide in your assembly until you face what you did wrong in splitting a church. Only after you renounce your sin, and seek forgiveness from God and your parent congregation, will you be victorious over these demonic influences.

"Wait," you say. "You're being harsh, Francis." No, I'm being honest. I am telling you what I have seen over and over again throughout the body of Christ. If you are the leader of a church that split from another group, listen to me carefully: You cannot justify criticism, gossip and division against your former pastor and then suppose those in your present church will not learn from your example. A leader will rise up who will be just like you. He will follow in your footsteps and use your approach to starting a church to justify his approach, only now it will be you suffering the split.

Jesus put it like this: "By your standard of measure, it will be measured to you" (Matt 7:2). Paul warned, "Do not be deceived, God is not mocked; for whatever a man sows, this he will also reap" (Gal 6:7). You cannot sow the wind without reaping the whirlwind (see Hos 8:7). God does not have to send meteors to punish us; sin carries its own punishment.

Indeed, although a splitting group launches into its future with songs of faith and joy, it is a baby marred by a birth defect. It is a church conceived by ambition and born in strife without the blessing of its parent. It may not happen immediately, but usually within three to five years it will suffer its own split and remain more vulnerable to splits than other churches.

You see, within the spiritual DNA of a split church there exists a hidden code, a programmed life pattern, which will continually reanimate each time an ambitious or critical leader rises in the group. Regardless of what doctrines the split church espouses about unity, the "encoded split pattern" exists in the marrow of the church. It is waiting for the right conditions to burst again into strife.

Let me say it again. Until the sin of division, of being part of a split, is acknowledged and then renounced; until forgiveness is sought from God and the offended congregation, the split pattern will always remain an option in your present church. You cannot sow the wind without reaping the whirlwind.

My advice is this: if you are currently involved in a division that is rapidly moving toward a split, stop immediately and seek arbitration from spiritual leaders you and the parent church respect. If you have been in a split and are part of the church that left, I urge you to contact your former church and ask for forgiveness. It may not be feasible to reunite; however, a time of forgiveness and prayer together between the two congregations, and perhaps partaking of communion—even praying the blessing of the Lord upon each other—will bring much healing and closure to the conflict.

If you were part of the parent church that suffered the split, there is no one who has suffered more during this time than your pastor. Within the first three months after the split, a time of honoring your pastor and his family will bring great healing to them and yourselves. It is also vital that you forgive the offending group, lest a root of bitterness spring up and many be defiled.

Some leaders feel there should be little or no contact between the two groups until a cooling off period passes. Emotions have been shredded, hearts are wounded and much misunderstanding exists. There is a time to talk and another time to turn to God and heal. This cooling off period should be a time to find new grace from God. If you lost people to a splintered group, there will be a temptation to continually focus on the past, wishing the division and split never happened. Yet, you cannot go forward while you are looking back. You need to refocus on the call and purpose of God for your church and press on. After you have forgiven the split group, give the entire matter to the Lord. What you give over, He will take over.

Even as you mourn the loss of friends, remember: Jesus Himself is praying, not only for healing but for oneness in the body of Christ. Letting go of the sorrow is as much a step of faith as trusting God to bring reconciliation.

Finally, in all things, you must let your love triumph. This is really about God expanding your capacity to show mercy. You must let this bad experience work for you. God is good and you must believe to see "the goodness of the Lord in the land of the living" (Ps 27:13).

Lord, in holy fear I come to You. I acknowledge before You that division is sin. I renounce participating in a carnal division and ask that You forgive me and those I may have wounded by my actions. I forgive those in the other group and ask, blessed Lord, that even in this You would perfect my heart. In Jesus' name. Amen.

PART FOUR:

BECOMING
CHRISTLIKE

*"The one who says he abides in Him
ought himself to walk
in the same manner as He walked."*
—1 John 2:6

CHAPTER FIFTEEN

TRUE SUCCESS

"That I may know Him, and the power of His resurrection and the fellowship of His sufferings, being conformed to His death; in order that I may attain to the resurrection from the dead" (Phil 3:10–11).

I n a real sense, this book is not about ending divisions, but the church becoming Christlike. Unity is the consequence of Christlikeness. If we have some goal other than conformity to Christ, we will inevitably be left vulnerable to deception and divisions.

When I speak of becoming Christlike, I mean a few specific things, such as humility, prayer, and possessing a mature, redemptive attitude of heart.

Beloved, all of us need to seek God for a true revelation of Christ's humility. Jesus said the humble were "greatest" in His kingdom (Matt18:4). We need in the church today, among leaders and congregations alike, the humility Jesus demonstrated when He girded Himself and washed His disciples' feet (see

John 13:4–5). This is not an imposed humility, but a choice we make as we seek the nature of the Savior.

We mentioned that one source of splits is ambition. However, when we make our goal the meekness of Christ, we know we can trust God with our future. Then we have no problem serving the vision and ministry of someone else along the way.

To seek Christlikeness means that, when I see something wrong in the born-again church, I am capable of looking at it maturely without panic. Because I am a person of prayer, I trust that God has a redemptive answer. Recall how Jesus handled the demon-possessed man in Gerasenes? The individual confronted Jesus as He passed among the tombs; broken chains dragged from his wrists and ankles. Yet, within minutes, Jesus had restored the man to his right mind, having delivered him of the tormenting evil spirits that possessed him (see Mark 5:1–15). The same Jesus who calmed the demoniac dwells in us. He doesn't want us to be swallowed up by what is wrong; He calls us to transform it.

Paul tells us to have in us the same attitude that we see in Christ who, existing in the form of God, did not regard His equality with the Father as a thing to be grasped, but He emptied Himself of His privileges and, in humility, took the form of a man—and then died for men (see Phil 2: 5–8)! In other words, Jesus saw the need—as terrible as it was—and came to redeem it. He could have simply destroyed the earth; He could have ignored our need. Instead He died for us. His footsteps are the will of God for me. With all my heart I desire to walk as He did: without fear, motivated by love, empowered to make a difference, and willing to die for those who would crucify me.

When I speak of becoming Christlike, it includes being submissive to authority. Jesus grew up in subjection to His parents; He insisted on submitting Himself to John's baptism, though He was clearly John's spiritual superior. He submitted Himself to the injustice of Pilate's secular authority, while entrusting Himself without fear to the power of the Father who judges righteously. Christ's eyes were not on Pilate but upon the Father who, in His omnipotence, would soon take every injustice and make it part of the plan of redemption. So, Jesus could submit to man because He had faith in God, the Father.

My call to you, beloved, is to walk as Christ walked, in humility and submission, so we can present to Him a church without spot or blemish or any such thing. Let us persevere in trials, knowing God sees and judges. Let us define success, not merely as having a name known on earth, but attaining Christlikeness and possessing a name known and honored in heaven.

Lord Jesus, I see in You all I want to be. I desire with all my heart to be like You, Lord. You have promised that a pupil shall become like his master. Fulfill Your promise in me! Transform me, that the world will see and worship You. Help me to define true success as attaining one goal: possessing Your glorious nature. Amen.

CHAPTER SIXTEEN

UNOFFENDABLE

"I will give you a new heart and put a new spirit within you; and I will remove the heart of stone from your flesh and give you a heart of flesh" (Ezek 36:26).

G od has a new heart for us that cannot be offended, an "unoffendable" heart. Beloved, possessing an unoffendable heart is not an option or a luxury; it's not a little thing. Consider: Jesus warns that, as we near the end of the age, a majority of people will be offended to such a degree that they fall away from the faith. Listen carefully to His warning:

> Then shall many be offended, and shall betray one another, and shall hate one another . . . and because iniquity shall abound, the love of many shall wax cold.
> —Matthew 24:10–12 KJV

"Many" will be offended; the love of "many" will grow cold. My prayer is that we will hear His words with holy fear.

When we allow an offense to remain in our hearts, it causes serious spiritual consequences. In the above verse Jesus named three dangerous results: betrayal, hatred and cold love. When we are offended with someone, even someone we care for, we must go to them. Otherwise, we begin to betray that relationship, talking maliciously behind their back to others, exposing their weaknesses and sins. We may mask our betrayal by saying we are just looking for advice or counsel, but when we look back, we see we have spoken negatively to far too many people. Our real goal was not to get spiritual help for ourselves but to seek revenge toward the one who offended us. How is such action not a manifestation of hatred? For an offended soul, cold love, betrayal and hatred go hand-in-hand.

People don't usually stumble over boulders; they stumble over stones, relatively small things. It may be that the personality of someone in authority bothers us and soon we are offended. Or, a friend or family member fails to meet our expectations, and we take an offense into our soul. Beloved, if we will "endure to the end," we will have to confront the things that bother us.

When Jesus warns that we need endurance, He is saying that it is easier to begin the race than finish it. Between now and the day you die, there will be major times of offense that you will need to overcome. You might be in such a time right now. Do not minimize the danger of harboring an offense.

No one plans on falling away; no one ever says, "Today, I think I'll try to develop a hardened, cold heart." Such things enter our souls through stealth and it is only naiveté that assumes it couldn't happen to us. I know many people who consistently become offended about one thing or another. Instead of dealing with the offenses, these people carry them until the weight disables their walk with God. You may be doing fine today, but I guarantee you, tomorrow something will happen that will inevitably disappoint or wound you; some injustice will strike you, demanding you retaliate in the flesh.

THE ROOT OF OFFENSE

An offense can strike at our virtues or sins, our values or our pride. It can penetrate and wound any dimension of the soul, both good and evil. I once brought a series of messages about gossip. Most people saw their sin and repented, but a core group of gossips were greatly offended and ultimately left the church. When the Holy Spirit exposes sin in someone's soul, if we refuse the opportunity to repent, we often become offended at the person who brought the teaching. Instead of humbling our hearts, we are outraged at the pastor or teachers in the church. Truthfully, most of the time, I have no idea who specifically needs to hear what I'm teaching, but God knows.

Paul told Timothy to "reprove, rebuke, exhort" (see 2 Tim 4:2). He didn't say, "exhort, exhort, exhort," but exhortation is what we receive in most churches. Certainly, we need to be encouraged, but there are also times, beloved, when we need to be reproved and rebuked. Today, there are preachers who are afraid to preach truth for fear people will react and leave the church. The end result is a church of easily offended people who cannot grow beyond their inability to accept correction.

People don't change by exhortation alone. There are areas in all of us that need to be confronted and disciplined. The pastor who refuses to discipline and correct those in sin is in disobedience to God. He is unable to lead people into any truly transforming changes in their lives; they will not "endure to the end" if they cannot be corrected (see Matt 24).

We need to become a people who say, "Lord, show me what needs to change in me." I'm talking about growing up. A wise man will receive a rebuke and he will prosper. But a fool rejects his father's discipline (see Prov 15:5).

PERSONAL OFFENSE

An offense can wound our pride when we are not recognized for our good works or ministry. This happened to my wife and I long ago while in California. We were young pastors at a conference when the main leader decided to personally greet each minister and wife. He greeted the couple on our right and then turned to his staff to ask a question. A moment later he returned, but passed us by and went to the couple on our left. Everyone around us saw we were bypassed. We were embarrassed and offended. But my wife wisely observed that we could allow this thing to hurt us or we could see it as an investment in sensitivity toward other people's feelings. The offense taught us how others feel when they are ignored. Do you see this? You must make that offense become an opportunity to become more Christlike.

The occasions for taking offense are practically endless. Indeed, we are daily given the opportunity to either be offended by something or to possess an unoffendable heart. The Lord's promise is that He's given us a new heart: a soft, entreatable heart that can be filled with His Spirit and abound with His love.

Lord, forgive me for being so easily offended and for carrying offenses. Father, my heart is foolish and weak. Grant me the unoffendable heart of Jesus Christ. Amen.

CHAPTER SEVENTEEN

NOTHING CAUSES THEM TO STUMBLE

"Then shall many be offended, and shall betray one an-other, and shall hate one another . . . and because iniquity shall abound, the love of many shall wax cold" (Matt 24:10–12 KJV).

I n the last chapter we looked at the lethal effect an offended spirit has upon our lives. We discussed how the only way to not be permanently offended was to attain the unoffendable heart of Jesus Christ.

Attaining Christ's heart is not a minor issue. Remember, Jesus warned that, in the last days, "many" would be offended. There is a difference between being wounded and being offended. We will frequently be wounded by an insensitive remark or injustice that occurs. But a "wounded spirit" is not the same thing as an "offended spirit." *An offended spirit occurs when we do not process our wounds in a Christlike manner.* Indeed, an offended spirit, left unattended and brooding in our minds, will soon manifest as betrayal, hatred and cold love. Jesus said offenses would be the ultimate cause that would lead many to fall from faith. Listen well: Jesus linked the real cause of apostasy not to wrong doctrines, but wrong reactions.

Aren't right doctrines important? Of course, but we can have right information and still have a wrong response. Doctrinal information can be upgraded and refined, but Proverbs warns that someone "offended is harder to be won than a strong city"; and "contentions" between people "are like the bars of a castle" (see Prov 18:19).

Yes, beware of false leaders, but more deceitful than false prophets or teachers are our own hearts when they are offended (see Jer 17:9). Are you living with an offended heart? If so, you are gradually slipping away from true Christianity, which is known for its agape love.

Thus, dealing with an offended heart is vital in maintaining ongoing spiritual maturity. For this reason, we need to look again at the things which offend us.

False Expectations

Sometimes offenses come because we expect *people* to fulfill our lives rather than *God*. Unrealistic or exaggerated expectations inevitably will cause others to fall short and offend us. Some desire their spouse or pastor or friends to meet their every need. God may, indeed, use people to help us. However, at the deepest level, our soul was created to find its security in God, not man. When the Almighty truly becomes our security, our peace flows from His love, wisdom and unlimited capabilities, and we can live comfortably with imperfect people around us.

Still, the very power of our expectations can choke out the sweetness of a personal relationship. Suppose that, instead of burdening people with our expectations, we simply learned to appreciate them for themselves—no strings attached. The fact is, our loved ones are not under any obligation to fulfill our desires. If they do fulfill them, it is their free choice, not our demands, that makes for a loving relationship.

Part of our problem is the affluent world we live in. We are served by hundreds of nonhuman "slaves," remarkable mechanical devices created just to serve us. Our slaves do laundry, clean dishes, figure bookkeeping and entertain us. They carry us across town and country—and for all they do, we are offended if their service does not meet or exceed our expectations.

Yet, your spouse, friends or pastor aren't your slaves. Our loved ones didn't come with money-back guarantees. We didn't buy them and we can't trade them for newer models. This may come as a shock, but we don't own our loved ones.

Some act as though they signed a contract with their spouse, such as they would with a carpenter or plumber—do such and such or you won't be paid. If you are an employer, a teacher or one who trains and holds people accountable, certain expectations are reasonable, but personal relationships are different. What I'm saying is this: What if, instead of expecting my spouse to love and serve me, I put the demand upon myself to love and serve her, no strings attached?

You say, but we said vows together. I expect my spouse to fulfill what was promised. What if she is fulfilling her vows to the best of her ability, but you can't even discern her efforts because you are looking for something else? I'm not saying there shouldn't be times when we openly and honestly talk about our relationships. Certainly, open communication would be helpful, but what if we put the weight of the burden to change upon ourselves instead of our spouse?

Jesus said the greatest among us would be servant of all. We, in our modern world, have things reversed—we are the ones who are supposed to be the slaves. It is only our pride that thinks otherwise.

Suppose that a husband, instead of expecting a full course dinner from his wife each night, learned to appreciate whatever she was able to offer him? Then, instead of his failed expectation becoming an offense, there would be a living, sincere appreciation for the food his wife prepared. I know we have arrangements by common consent, but in reality, a wife is under no obligation to cook special meals or do housekeeping. You did not marry her to be your housekeeper, but to become one with her.

Or imagine a husband who works at a long, tiring job. However, his wife expects that he will work another two hours at home or go shopping with her or listen attentively about her problems. What if, instead, she welcomed him at the door and sincerely thanked him for daily giving himself to support their family? What if she met him, not with demands, but with appreciation? Maybe she would even rub his shoulders when he came home and, because of love, prepare his favorite meal.

You see, expectations can seem to be legitimate parts of a relationship, but they can also cause us to be offended and disappointed when people fall short. We should approach personal relationships with only one expectation: to serve—a demand we should put upon ourselves, not others. Let us expect of ourselves to always show love and thanksgiving for whatever we receive from our loved ones. Beloved, if we did so, we would have many happy couples in our midst.

IN THE CHURCH

I am speaking of family relationships because the church is a family. If we as pastors and churches learned to appreciate each other without false expectations, we would see great healing come to our congregations.

Yes, it is important that leaders themselves be equipped, encouraged, and held accountable. However, pastors also need certain freedoms to guide their churches. Indeed, the vision of a local church resides principally in the office of the senior pastor. He may answer to a church board or district supervisor, but God puts a special grace in the pastor, which is given him to lead the church. This imperfect man, together with his leadership team, is the Lord's primary means of guiding the congregation.

However, when we expect the pastor to act like someone we saw on Christian television, it cannot help but breed discontent, false expectations and offenses. When our pastor resists these expectations, often he is simply seeking to be true to the vision he feels the Lord has given him. When the discontented individuals react, an oppression is released against that leader that actually feels and works like witchcraft (see 1 Sam 15:23).

This happened to me a number of years ago. Several people in the church began praying that I would become more like a famed television minister. Each week they sat right in the front row, critically comparing me to the famous teacher they enjoyed. These people were not evil; they were good Christians, but their disappointment with me was a source of oppression that stole my confidence and actually lessened my effectiveness.

Let me give you an example from the Bible: Elisha succeeded Elijah, yet initially he failed the expectations of the sons of the prophets. They were familiar with Elijah's ministry style. However, Elisha seemed to be Elijah's opposite. The prophets asked Elisha to send them to find Elijah. Perhaps he wasn't dead, but only "on some mountain" (2 Kings 2:16). Elisha refused. The next verse says that they "urged him until he was ashamed." Of what was Elisha ashamed? Even though he had received a double portion of Elijah's spirit, he became ashamed that he was not more like Elijah.

Our failed expectations can make our pastor feel ashamed for who he is. Nothing will kill the flowing of the Holy Spirit like ongoing criticisms of your church leaders. Learn to appreciate them for the gifts God has given them; pray for them, that they may become more like Christ.

Remember, if your pastor is faithful to preach the gospel week in and out, if he serves the Lord by trying to minister to Christ's church, then God accepts him and you should honor him. He is a gift from God.

Likewise, pastors, accept and love the flock where the Lord has placed you. Don't compare them to other churches, but appreciate their uniqueness in God's eyes. These people will cause you to grow in ways you haven't grown before, so thank God for them.

The psalmist wrote, "Those who love Thy law have great peace, and nothing causes them to stumble" (Ps 119:165). There is a place in God where, as we mature, we can possess Christ's perfect response to all things. If we, as pastors and congregations, put away false, unrealistic expectations and focus on becoming Christlike to one another, we will have great peace. Beloved, nothing will cause us to stumble.

Lord, grant me that new creation heart that can walk as Jesus walked, through a world of offenses, without stumbling. I want to see everything as an opportunity to pray, everything as an opportunity to become Christlike. Lord help me to interpret offenses as opportunities that lead to transformations. Grant me, Lord Jesus, the pulse and beat of Your unoffendable heart. Amen.

CHAPTER EIGHTEEN

SATAN'S HOUR

There is no greater opportunity to become Christlike than in the midst of pain and injustice. When Satan is raging with evil, God is planning to turn it to good. If we maintain our integrity in battle; if we let love rise to its purest expression, we will touch the heart of God. Such is the path to God's power.

A s we near the end of this book, my prayer is that we will have eliminated a number of the vulnerabilities to, and effects of, church splits and other ungodly divisions. At the same time, I realize that we can do almost everything right as pastors and churches and still suffer divisions. For some of us, this may actually be part of God's greater plan for our lives—that we should endure rejection, conflict and slander as part of the process of truly becoming Christlike.

A COLLECTIVE MADNESS

Let me speak once more to you who may be part of a group engaged in splitting a church. My earnest admonition is that you flee quickly from the dividing group. For once you fully embrace the resolve to split your church, a type of "collective madness" occurs. You will know what you are doing is wrong, but will become so hardened that you detach yourself from guilt. You will be aware that your anger is venomous and unchristlike, but you will be powerless to mute your words.

Beloved, no one needs to slay love to defend truth. Love is not truth's enemy; it is its validator. If what you say cannot be said in love, do not say it. It is not of God. To speak without love is evidence that the collective madness has begun to infect your soul.

SATAN'S HOUR

Let us isolate this terrible insanity that drives people to say and do things they know are wrong. Jesus Himself, during His last few days on earth, watched this invasion from hell advance upon the people of Jerusalem, infecting even His own disciples.

For the sake of discernment, we shall call this season of madness "Satan's hour." It is a period of time when the restraining powers of all that is good seem to withdraw from human relationships. Instead of love, or even civility, what governs the dissenting group is the manifest "power of darkness" (see Luke 22:53). It is as though people invite the legions of hell to depart the abode of the damned and find access to their secret resentments—the unresolved issues that exist in their hearts. Those things that are evil within human nature are fully awakened, and then empowered by hell to fulfill every demonic gratification.

This collective madness is the exact opposite of a visitation from heaven; it is a visitation from hell. It is not the healing of bodies, but the wounding of hearts. It is not reconciliation between souls, but estrangement of friends. It is not truth spoken in love, but emotions discharged in wrath. It is not the gospel of peace, but the heartache of strife. During Satan's hour, friends become enemies; loyalties become betrayals; and unity degrades into unreconcilable division. Satan's hour is an uncontested, seemingly unstoppable, invasion from hell, where every hidden jealousy, every secret, unresolved bitterness in the human heart is unsheathed and used as a weapon in the hands of demons of strife.

If we study the terrible, demonic events which were compressed into Jesus' last earthly days, we can gain a vital insight into the demonic activity in church splits; more importantly, we can see how God can bring victory through it.

First, this swarm of evil did not take Jesus unaware. Throughout the time of His ministry Jesus frequently warned His disciples that a time of unfettered evil would come (see Mark 8:31; 9:12; Luke 17:25). As the day arrived, Jesus announced to His disciples that the prince of darkness was coming (John 14:30). Yet, knowing a time of satanic darkness was at hand did not make enduring it easier; knowing such a time was imminent, however, did help Jesus to prepare.

Thus, Jesus was fully aware that, during Satan's hour, evil would strike in full force and His disciples would be sifted severely (see Luke 22:31); His followers would scatter, and one of the twelve would betray Him. Indeed, even His closest friends would deny they ever knew Him (see Luke 22:60–61). Satan's hour was a time when reality itself seemingly bent in service to the power of darkness (Luke 22:53), and the Father offered nothing Jesus could use to stop it.

We cannot help but picture Jesus always upbeat and overcoming, but when hell was unleashed, even God's Son was not invulnerable to Satan's oppression. "Grieved and distressed," Jesus took His closest friends aside and spoke intimately with them about His heartache.

"My soul is deeply grieved, to the point of death," He said, as He urged His closest friends, Peter, James and John, to keep watch with Him. Yet, the heaviness of satanic battle overwhelmed them. Even John, who had rested his head on Jesus' breast, could not lift his head from slumber—all escaped into sleep, hiding themselves from excessive sorrow (see Matt 26:38–45).

Staggered by the weight of the spiritual attack against Him, Jesus "fell to the ground, and began to pray that if it were possible, the hour might pass Him by" (Mark 14:35). We know Jesus ministered peace wherever He went, yet now His intense, internal struggle ruptured blood vessels on His face, which beaded on His skin. Again, He sought to waken His disciples. Roused from their sleep, they saw the droplets of blood on His brow and cheeks; still, they could not endure.

I think it is significant that Jesus, so familiar with simply trusting His Father in all things, returned to His friends three times during the hour of His Gethsemane prayer (see Matt 26:39–45). Beloved, there are some agonies in life for which God alone seems not enough; we crave also the comfort of our friends (see Prov 17:17). There is no substitute for God, yet our soul also needs the embrace of a loyal companion, the shoulder of a faithful friend who has become closer than a brother.

Yet, Jesus' friends were not there for Him. They slept while He prayed. They fled when the Pharisees came (see Matt 26:56). During the trial when, of all people, they could have certainly defended Jesus' character and doctrine, they hid. Even if others would forsake Him, surely these who broke bread with Him, who knew His heart, would speak in His defense. Yet from Gethsemane to the cross, Jesus heard the voice of just one friend. It was Peter's, who less than a day earlier had sworn undying loyalty, swearing now he never knew Him (see Matt 26:69–70; Luke 22:61).

Our Master experienced betrayal, abandonment, slander, mockery and gross injustice. He endured the heartache of His disciples' failures—their failure to pray, failure to stand and failure to defend the truth about their most wonderful friend and Lord.

Dear follower of Jesus, what our Messiah endured and what the disciples suffered, in various degrees, are all the elements found in a church split. What happens to a pastor—what might have happened to *your* pastor during a church split—is similar in nature to what Jesus Himself suffered in His last few days.

HOW JESUS OVERCAME

For a pastor, there exists only one way out of the tragedy of a church split: become like Jesus. You see, God's greatest goal for our lives is not that we become successful ministers, but that we become Christlike. Pastoring is simply an opportunity to be transformed into Christlikeness. Now, this does not mean we must die for the sins of the world, but it does mean that, when we go through injustices and conflicts, Christ must be manifested in our mortal lives.

What I mean by "manifesting Christ in our lives" is that we learn to respond to the human failures in our world as Jesus did in His. There are three sources of wounding that come to a minister during a split. The first is the failure of friends or church members to speak up in his defense or to persevere, on his behalf, in prayer. Confusion and fear, suspicion and doubt overshadow people who know better, paralyzing them into inaction. To counteract the failure of His disciples, and knowing they too were being sifted, Jesus assured them, "but I have prayed for you, that your faith may not fail; and you, when once you have turned again, strengthen your brothers" (Luke 22:32).

There are valuable lessons for Jesus' disciples that only failure can teach, and Jesus knew this. These disciples had been arguing among themselves which of them might be the greatest; now they were humbled, broken and contrite enough for God to use them. God used their failure to excavate their souls of pride; now emptied, they were capable of being filled with the Holy Spirit. These same disciples would soon be willing to suffer and die for Jesus, and count it an honor to do so. They never denied

Him again. Knowing they would fail Him, Jesus prayed that during their trial their faith would not fail and, upon returning, they would become a strength for others.

For the disciples, their biggest problem was carrying the burden of their failure; their guilt and condemnation weighed heavily upon them. Yet, immediately after warning them that they would, in fact, each deny Him, Jesus comforted them, "Let not your heart be troubled" (see John 13:38–14:1). Incredibly, even before they fell, Jesus sought to remove the weight of condemnation that would inevitably seek to overwhelm them.

So, pastors, as Jesus loved His disciples, even though they failed Him, so we need to love those who, though falling short of our expectations, still remain with us. They will strengthen others. We need to remove any sense of condemnation or blame from those who have disappointed us. As they see our Christlike reactions, they too will become united to serve God's highest purposes.

HOW JESUS HANDLED HIS ENEMIES

Jesus loved His disciples and His love brought them through. However, the next people we must deal with are those playing the role of the enemy, those who were instruments of injustice, who sought to destroy a ministry through gossip and slander. We must find Christ's reaction to these and emulate His behavior.

While we may have many legitimate arguments to wage against our accusers, Jesus stood silently before His. Beloved, there is a time to take your stand and defend what God is doing, and there is a time to become silent and simply entrust yourself to God. Peter reveals how Jesus processed the storm of accusation that came against His soul. Peter writes, "while being reviled, He did not revile in return; while suffering, He uttered no threats, but kept entrusting Himself to Him who judges righteously" (1 Peter 2:23).

If your words will not persuade your attackers, beloved, recognize it is time to be silent. Yet, Jesus was not just silent; He bore their sins on His cross (see 1 Peter 2:24). So also for us: It is not enough that we not react negatively; we must respond positively to those who come against us, just as Christ did. We must pray the mercy prayer, even when it may appear that they have successfully put to death our vision.

You see, Jesus knew Satan's hour was coming. Yet He also knew that if He could maintain His vision of redemption and His capacity to love, it would be through this very time of darkness that redemption would triumph for mankind. So, though grieved and deeply troubled, Jesus prayed, "What shall I say, 'Father, save Me from this hour'? But for this purpose I came" (John 12:27).

Jesus understood that for redemption to be accomplished, His love would face its most severe test. Jesus knew this battle was over one thing: would He allow love to reach full maturity and its most perfect expression? Would He maintain His passion for man's redemption even as men mocked and crucified Him?

So it is with us. God allows injustices to perfect our love. The cross is the cost we pay so love can triumph. This battle is not about you and your enemies, but about you maintaining love in the midst of injustice.

Dear pastor, let us redefine our meaning of success. Here is the success that will bring the power of redemption into our world: When we have endured Satan's hour and, instead of reacting, allowed adversity to refine our love, we will have succeeded in the purpose of our existence.

Beloved, regardless of the test God calls you to endure, it is not about you and your relational opponent. The real issue is about you and God. Will you allow love to be perfected? Will you transform Satan's hour into an offering of your life in Christlike surrender?

Lord Jesus, my soul longs and even yearns to be like You. Master of all that is good, grant me grace to succeed in love. Guard my heart from its natural instinct for self-survival. Let me never choose the way of hardness; let me, in all things, find the way of life. Even now, I offer myself for those who have struck me. Thank You for the opportunity to become like You. Amen.

THE DECEPTION SURROUNDING SPLITS

The Bible has a great deal to say about unity. However, I have yet to find one New Testament example where the Scriptures encourage born-again Christians to divide from each other. The Lord *multiplied* the church and *added* to their numbers; He did not divide His people.

LET THE WORD BE TRUE

For over thirty years I have witnessed many Scriptures taken out of context and twisted to suit the purpose of division. Yet, if we simply read objectively, we will not find one place where the Spirit of God inspired a faction within a church to divide and start another group, even if the first group was imperfect.

Dividing a church has no scriptural precedent. Just as people are deceived in their motives when they divide Christ's church, so they are deceived when they read the Scriptures seeking to justify themselves.

For instance, I have frequently heard quoted Paul's admonition, "Come out from their midst and be separate" (2 Cor 6:17). However, the apostle was not speaking of being separated from other Christians. Rather, his purpose was to warn Christians about being "unequally yoked" with pagans or "unbelievers" (see 2 Cor 6:14–15 KJV).

Interestingly, the Old Testament version of this same verse was used by the Pharisees to justify their condescending attitude toward other Jews. In fact, the name *Pharisee* literally translated means "the separate." Jesus warned of those who "trusted in themselves that they were righteous, and viewed others with contempt" (Luke 18:9). This attitude of self-righteous contempt is often what motivates a faction to think of itself as more spiritual than another, and thus justify being "separate."

Another historic misinterpretation comes from First Corinthians, chapter 11, where Paul seems to concede that splits and divisions were almost necessary. He wrote: "I hear that divisions exist among you; and in part, I believe it. For there must also be factions among you, in order that those who are approved may have become evident among you" (1 Cor 11:18b–19).

Certainly, isolated by itself, the idea that there "must also be factions . . . that those who are approved may have become evident" adds legitimacy to the idea of splits and divisions. Of course, those who split from others always identify themselves as "those who are approved."

However, the actual context of the verse reveals the apostle's true perception and view. Here's the complete eighteenth verse: "For, in the first place, when you come together as a church, I hear that divisions exist among you; and in part, I believe it" (1 Cor 11:18).

Listen carefully to Paul's backdrop of unity upon which he isolates the problem of divisions. He introduces his thoughts by saying, "When you come together as a church . . ." Don't rush past his opening address. They hadn't split from each other; they were not meeting in different buildings, each with a unique name on a corner sign. They were still united and they all still would "come together as a church." In fact, until the split between Constantinople and Rome two hundred years later, there was only the one Christian church.

Paul wasn't justifying the divisions among them. In fact, the primary theme of First Corinthians is to reestablish unity (see chapters 1, 3, 8, 10:16–24, 11, 12, 13, 14). He wrote specifically to *correct* their divisions. But even though, in their carnality, some were followers of Paul while others followed Apollos or Cephas, they still came "together as a church." Paul's goal in this letter was to get them to see past the leaders who brought them into the kingdom and look at the King!

Every week the Christians in Corinth met together for worship, a love feast and weekly communion. It was here, in the administration of food, that they had broken into the cliques and factions that Paul identified as "approved." Some, indeed, tried to keep their focus on the significance of the Lord's Supper, while others were devouring as much as they could during the community meal (see 1 Cor 11:20–22, 33–34)!

In no way had Paul suddenly altered his course and decided that divisions were not a bad thing after all. Rather, he was acknowledging that the more gluttonous Christians had become a separate group within the church. In contrast, the Christians who reverently waited unintentionally became a group as well. This was not by premeditated design or organizational intent, but by their self-discipline and composure. Just as cream rises to the top of milk, so within the church there were those whose spirituality gave contrast to the carnality of others—and those were the ones who were approved. But they didn't divide from the others and form a new church within the church. Paul didn't urge them to separate from the others, for they all still "came together as a church."

Indeed, in the very next chapter, Paul reiterates his theme of unity, using the analogy of a body that is diverse, yet interdependently united. Everything he has written to this point is captured in his summary-thought in verse 25. Listen again to his heart:

> That there should be no schism in the body; but that the members should have the same care one for another.
>   —1 Corinthians 12:25 KJV

Beloved, the word translated "schism" in the King James (rendered "division" in the NAS), means "split" in the Greek language. Translated literally, Paul is saying "there should be no split in the body."

What part of "no" don't we understand? Unity is the central theme of First Corinthians. How could one honestly ignore entire chapters about unity and take one half-verse out of context to justify a split? (1 Cor 11:18–19) This is willful deception.

THE GOAL IS UNITY

In all that the New Testament declares for Christians—in all of the epistles and pastoral letters of Paul and the other apostles—the call is clearly, unmistakably toward unity, not division. There was a hurricane of spiritual wind blowing and bending the church in the direction of oneness with each other in Christ. The repeated rebuke comes because of disunity and sectarianism.

Another verse used to justify splitting a church comes from Jesus Himself. He said, "Do you suppose that I came to grant peace on earth? I tell you, no, but rather division" (Luke 12:51). Jesus is not talking about dividing His people, but dividing those who follow Him from those who do not. Jesus does indeed separate us from the world, however He eternally unites us to Himself and one another.

As I searched through the New Testament on the subject of Christian unity, there were literally hundreds of verses pointing toward oneness in the born-again church. After years of study on this subject, I have yet to read one verse that instructed a group of Christians to slander, divide and split from another group of Christians in a city, just because that other group was imperfect. If God's Word calls us to unity with other born-again Christians throughout an entire city, how much more does this same command apply to relationships in a local church?

Yet, we need to realize that we are all different, with differing strengths and passions. Part of unity means we can accept that some people within our church community may desire to function differently than others. This diversity need not become disunity. We must defend the right to be unique, with differing tasks. Yet, diversity must find its expression without contention or strife.

The test for leaders and congregations is to find creative ways to facilitate diversity while remaining united. If unity of purpose cannot be maintained within a body of people, a church plant born of love and done with wisdom in the Lord's timing is a creative possibility.

ONE EXAMPLE

Several years ago I approached one of our associate pastors at River of Life, Marty Boller, and asked if he was praying about moving out of state. He said, "Yes." Marty had been a Vineyard pastor who merged his congregation with us and now, seven years later, he wanted to return to the Vineyard association of churches. Yet Marty did not want to sow division in our community, so he planned on moving to Canada to start his church!

Because he was an honorable man and very committed to unity, I suggested he take a few months and explain his vision in a weekly class with those from our church who were interested. When Marty started a new work in our city, he did so with a dozen or so River of Life families, and others. Today, we remain great friends and serve together in many citywide projects. We are closer because he was patient, wise and non-divisive.

There are many creative ways to multiply a church as long as we stay Christlike. It's when pride or ambition enter that division soon follows.

A Purer First Century Church?

The argument arises that the church was much purer in its early years than it is now—so today we need to separate from others because of sin in the camp. The church in Jerusalem, in its inception, certainly set a standard for us all. However, as the church expanded to other cities and cultures, there were many problems; in some cases, their failures were worse than our own. Yet, the apostles who served Christ's church still called for unity in spite of the churches' imperfections.

Even in Jesus' address to the seven churches in the Revelation of John, though sin existed in the churches in five cities, Christ never instructed the innocent to break from the sinners. Rather, He commended those who walked in purity and left them in the midst of the sinful as an example of His righteousness.

Doctrine

Another argument used to justify splits has to do with doctrinal interpretation. Let me make it clear that our doctrines are very important—they define our belief systems and open the door to spiritual realities and levels of blessedness of which we would be otherwise ignorant. Having clear biblically based doctrines also provide boundaries to keep us from deception and half truths.

However, there are both core truths and peripheral truths to our faith. There are precepts that we must be willing to die for, yet there are other instructions that good Christians interpret differently. Because we are all learning, we must be willing to yield and stay humble.

In practical terms, we cannot be united with those who do not believe in the deity of Christ. Yet, we certainly can maintain the unity of the spirit, for instance, with someone who has a different view about the timing of the rapture. We cannot dilute God's truth concerning the new covenant, the inspiration of the Scriptures, the centrality of Jesus Christ, the atonement of His cross, His bodily resurrection, His physical return, salvation by grace through faith, the Trinity and the indwelling work of the Holy Spirit. But we are still learning about spiritual gifts, effective church government, signs and wonders, styles of praise, and various programs that train youth and make disciples of adults.

When Jesus defined the requirements for unity in John 17, He said our oneness would arise from three core realities. He said spiritual oneness would come as we believed in His name, His Word and His glory (John 17:11, 20–22). These fundamental truths, if adhered to, He said, would unite His people.

However, to split a church because of a disagreement concerning peripheral doctrines is a smoke screen. It is a deception. There are those who argue they are taking their stand in defense of God's Word. Yet, how can they divide a church in defiance of God's Word? A person who will split a church over a nonfundamental doctrine or over a spiritual gift or style of worship is deceived and seeking to deceive others.

Lord, forgive us for accepting divisions. Heal Your church, O God! Bring us into Christ-centered unity, that the world would believe in Your power. Amen.

QUESTIONS AND ANSWERS

WHAT EXACTLY IS A CHURCH SPLIT?

Generally speaking, a split occurs when a group within a church, usually under the influence of an associate minister or worship leader, finds fault with the senior pastor's leadership. Usually, the goal of the dissenting group is not merely change, but control of the church. They are seeking power. If they cannot gain control of the church, they refine their organization, solidify their constituency and, without the blessing of the parent church, leave to start a new church in the community.

IS THE PASTOR EVER AT FAULT IN A SPLIT?

Yes. A split may occur when a church board hires (or "extends a call" to) a pastor whom they think will serve the vision of the church. If the church has been established for a number of years, and the founding minister is no longer involved, there exists a unique authority within the church board. In a sense, the deacons or elders serve that church as the "keepers of the vision." They are looking to maintain consistency between past leaders and present leaders. They expect change, but also expect that the pastor who answers their call will respect their preferences.

Splits often occur when a minister hides his convictions concerning certain doctrines or spiritual gifts. Then, when the board realizes this pastor has not been forthright with his intentions, the pastor either resigns or is fired. Unfortunately, there is usually a certain percentage of the church that has bonded with the pastor and may decide to leave with him to begin a new work in the same community. This is an unethical way to start a church.

Additionally, if a pastor falls into serious sin, yet refuses to submit to discipline, the other leaders in that church have a moral responsibility to remove that pastor. If he refuses to submit to the church board, the elders of that church might start a new work, splitting from the pastor and those loyal to him. They have not sinned by leaving the pastor who refuses correction.

Another occasion when a split might become necessary occurs when the leaders of a denomination fall away from the faith and seek to spread their apostasy into their denomination. If senior church leaders deny the deity of Christ or find no problem ordaining and endorsing homosexuals, or if they teach that all religions lead to God, this is a denomination that has turned its back on biblical Christianity. For a pastor to withdraw his congregation from that denomination is not sin, but a noble responsibility.

However, I would also suggest that, before pulling out of that denomination, local church leadership seek out other pastors who are likewise resisting the downward spiral of their denomination. Perhaps there are pockets of godly pastors within the denomination who are also combating the current trend away from godliness. Still, to withdraw from the denomination as a means of protest, especially to protect Christ's sheep, can be an honorable decision.

WHAT ABOUT LEAVING A CHURCH; WOULD THAT BE CONSIDERED SPLITTING?

If a person, family or even up to three or four families decided to transfer to another church, their actions should not be considered a split. We will always have people coming and going, needing to be equipped by the variety of ministers Christ has throughout His church. People should be free to sense and fulfill the changing seasons in their lives. But they should make their transition with a minimum of rancor or contention. They should also be careful not to sow discontentment at their former church. Whenever possible, pastors should make a church transfer a positive experience for all, sending attenders to their next church with a blessing.

In the New Testament, apparently "letters of commendation" often accompanied Christians as they traveled between churches or cities (see 2 Cor 3:1). Communication is important. Today, a simple phone call between pastors will do. If we are members of a church and plan on relocating to another church, it is simply a courtesy to communicate to your pastors and staff that you are moving on. However, to leave one congregation and go to another is part of our liberty in Christ.

ARE THERE TIMES OF GREATER BATTLE?

There will always be certain times when we are more vulnerable to strife and division. Indeed, one such time occurs when a congregation is in a season of change. Trying to adjust to a new pastor or church training program calls for greater grace; a new worship leader may sing your favorite chorus differently, or the deacon board's new building plan strikes you wrong. Even times of sudden growth can be disturbing to some, leaving them vulnerable to criticism and withdrawal.

Whatever the current transition is, there will always be those who think the old ways were better. In nearly every church, there will be "those who desire change" sitting side-by-side with "those who hate change." God puts both types of people in the same congregation to create flexibility and balance in all.

Yet, as difficult as the transition is, remember: Satan will seek opportunities for division and strife. This is why we should honor our church leaders and pray for them. Their pace rarely pleases everyone.

WHAT ABOUT THE BIBLICAL ADMONITION TO GOD'S PEOPLE TO COME OUT OF BABYLON? (REV 17)

My focus is about the relationship evangelical Christians have with one another, not Babylon. Within the born-again, Christ-trusting congregation of God, church splits are a sin that needs to be renounced.

OUR CHURCH SPLIT OVER "SIGNS AND WONDERS."

Spiritual phenomena should never be a reason a church divides, yet often the enemy is able to manipulate human reactions and use our own "sensibilities" against us. Certainly, the ministry of prayer for God's people is consistent with the ministry of Jesus Himself. It is all the more powerful when God *answers* prayer with renewed spirits, minds and bodies. Let us defend laying hands upon the sick and praying for them. However, when certain signs begin to manifest, it is easy to "ritualize" the phenomena. The more extra-biblical in nature that phenomena is, the more likely Satan will make it divisive.

Generally speaking, a spiritual phenomenon can be categorized as that which is either biblical, extra-biblical, or unbiblical. The manifestations accompanying New Age concepts, astrology, obsession with UFOs, "channeling," witchcraft, and the like are obviously unbiblical. The Bible condemns these things, since the spiritual activity joined to them is demonic.

Biblical manifestations include anointed preaching (resulting in conviction, repentance, or inspiration in the listener); physical or emotional healing; deliverance from demonic possession, and the inspired "word" gifts: prophecy, tongues, words of knowledge and wisdom (see 1 Cor 12, 14). However, even in the first century, conflict arose with the misuse of spiritual gifts. Although spiritual gifts are biblical in nature, their content should be tested against Scripture, their presentation should be done decently and in order, and any word of direction should be confirmed by two or three witnesses.

While the Lord is most clearly recognized in biblical manifestations, and most obviously not associated with what is unbiblical, difficulty comes when we encounter religious manifestations which have no pattern in the Bible. These would be classified as extra-biblical, and it is around these signs that churches most often split.

I am not going to pass judgment on the legitimacy of any extra-biblical sign. I know a great many pastors who were personally restored during a time of spiritual renewal in which the Lord used an extra-biblical sign; I also know pastors who suffered severe nervous breakdowns because of the strife they experienced as they tried to shepherd a congregation through the turbulence generated by extra-biblical signs. I will simply suggest that, as pastors, after introducing the spiritual phenomena to your church over a period of several weeks, you add a monthly or biweekly Friday evening service that is geared just for this renewal, without seeking to conform your whole congregation to it. This way people will not be forced to be "with it" or "against it."

Speaking as one who has been in ministry for over thirty years, the spiritual phenomena will not be manifest in a congregation forever. You cannot build your church on signs and wonders. You must preach the Word and disciple your congregation. Make them followers of Jesus. If you are attending a church where making disciples of Jesus is the pastor's goal, do not split or divide that church over signs.

OUR CHURCH STARTED YEARS AGO AS A RESULT OF A SPLIT. WE HAVE SINCE SUFFERED FOUR SPLITS OURSELVES AND ARE CURRENTLY IN ANOTHER ONE. HOW DO WE BREAK THIS CURSE?

I suggest that you contact the original church yours split from and arrange a time when you can meet with the pastor. Together with your leadership team, ask him and his leaders for forgiveness for how your church was started. See if you can arrange to have a joint meeting between the two churches where the past can be forgiven and brought to the cross. You might also have communion together and pledge to be one another's keeper. Make sure your congregation is fully aware of your repentance so they can join with you in breaking the pattern of division.

WHEN A PASTOR IS A CONTROLLING PERSONALITY, HOW DO YOU LEAVE?

I am comforted by the fact that heaven is a big place with room for all sorts of people. For some of us, it is hard to accept, but there are many who genuinely thrive under strict leadership. Certain people need clear rules, and a leader who communicates with strong authority is a help to them. Others, of course, feel completely smothered by this type of leader. They also find it difficult to leave without feeling excessive guilt or intimidation.

First, remember, you are free in Jesus. No man on earth is your lord, and your pastor is your servant. You are completely at liberty to visit other places of worship. When you have found a new church home, contact your former pastor, thank him, and just move on as best you can.

If, however, the pastor is so controlling that he warns you that you will lose your salvation if you leave, or he threatens you with subtle curses, contact another pastor in your community and get counsel. You do not have to submit to such abuse, and neither should anyone else in that church.

If new wine must be put in new wineskins, it seems to me that sometimes splits are inevitable.

Again, I think we need Jesus as our pattern. Jesus didn't slander John the Baptist and work people out of his movement, which is what happens in a church split. In fact, when John's disciples saw that Jesus was baptizing more people than John, and the Pharisees noticed the opportunity for strife, Jesus moved His ministry elsewhere, lest he cause division in the kingdom of God (see John 2). As best as I can tell, Jesus' other disciples were unattached to any group or movement in Israel. Jesus did not split a group to start His work; He is the pattern for the "new wine."

Recently, our pastor (and his staff) came under a lot of criticism from the church board and were suddenly fired. Over the past years he had built our congregation to twice the size it first was. We have since started a new church, and he is still our pastor, but I was wondering, was starting a new church wrong?

Assuming there was no serious sin involved, the dismissal of a pastoral staff seems harsh. I would encourage them, as the Lord leads and confirms the timing, to look for ways to heal the wounds between both groups. The best outcome of this situation is for each congregation to accept and respect each other's different preferences and forgive each other. Perhaps the Lord will provide a time when both groups can meet together with the Lord's Supper. To speak the blessing of the Lord over each other and release one another from the heartache of the past will go far in establishing healing.

MY PASTOR'S SERMONS HAVE BEEN DRY AND LIFELESS FOR QUITE AWHILE. WHEN WE ARE NOT BEING FED THE MEAT OF GOD'S WORD, SHOULD WE START OUR OWN CHURCH?

No teacher brings sermons that are "meat." Jesus said that His "meat" was to do the will of His Father. If your church seems dry and you are hungry for meat, I suggest you begin doing the will of God in your church. What I mean is that you start a prayer group for your pastor. Encourage him with comments about his sermon. Perhaps send him words of encouragement and build him up.

You say, "But this is what we want him to do for us." If you pray for him, more than likely he will begin to gain new confidence and become a great encouragement to you. But the real "meat" is this: see the need and be mature enough in Christ to pray, to encourage and to stand in faith until that need is met by the Holy Spirit.

For more questions and answers, please visit our web site at http://www.inchristsimage.org.